Python for Web Development: Build Dynamic Websites with Django

A Step-by-Step Guide to Mastering Python for Web Development

MIGUEL FARMER

RAFAEL SANDERS

Table of Content

TABLE OF CONTENTS

INTRODUCTION

Mastering Django: From Basics to Advanced Features

Welcome to *Mastering Django: From Basics to Advanced Features*, your comprehensive guide to learning and mastering Django, one of the most powerful and popular web development frameworks in Python. Whether you are just starting your journey in web development or are looking to expand your knowledge with advanced concepts, this book is designed to provide you with a thorough understanding of Django's core principles and beyond.

Django is known for its "batteries-included" philosophy, offering developers a full suite of tools to build scalable, secure, and maintainable web applications. From rapid prototyping to building complex, production-ready systems, Django's rich ecosystem allows developers to focus on building unique features while Django handles the heavy lifting of things like authentication, database management, URL routing, and more. This book aims to provide a well-rounded understanding of Django that will allow you to take full advantage of its potential.

Who Should Read This Book?

This book is suitable for a wide range of developers:

- **Beginners**: If you're new to web development or have minimal experience with Django, you'll find this book approachable. It will take you through the essential concepts step-by-step, starting with setting up your first Django project and understanding its core components.
- **Intermediate Developers**: If you already have some Django experience and are familiar with basic concepts like models, views, and templates, this book will deepen your knowledge and introduce you to advanced features like Django Channels, Celery, and performance optimization techniques.
- **Experienced Developers**: If you're already proficient with Django, this book will provide valuable insights into best practices, performance scaling, and integrating complex features such as real-time web apps, background task processing, and customizing Django's admin interface.

What Will You Learn?

Throughout this book, we will guide you through the process of building robust, real-world applications with Django. From the foundational concepts to the more advanced capabilities, we'll cover a wide range of topics that will equip you to build sophisticated web applications.

- **Foundational Concepts**: We'll start by helping you set up a Django project and guide you through the creation of models, views, and templates. You'll learn how to work with Django's ORM, handle forms, and make use of Django's admin interface.

- **Real-World Applications**: You will learn how to build complete, functional applications. This includes everything from planning an app, defining data models, and handling user authentication, to implementing complex business logic and building dynamic user interfaces.

- **Advanced Django Features**: We'll delve into Django's advanced features, including asynchronous programming with Django Channels, background task processing with Celery, and real-time web applications. You will also learn how to optimize the performance of your Django applications with caching, database indexing, and load balancing.

- **Customization**: As your applications grow, you'll need to customize Django's behavior to fit your specific needs. You will learn how to customize the Django admin interface, extend Django with third-party libraries and APIs, and work with Django signals and middleware.

- **Deployment and Maintenance**: Finally, this book will teach you the best practices for deploying your Django applications to production, maintaining your codebase, handling database migrations, and scaling your application to handle increasing traffic.

How This Book Is Organized

This book is structured to take you from beginner to expert in a systematic way, with practical examples and exercises along the way.

1. **Getting Started with Django**: The first chapters will help you set up Django, build your first models, views, and templates, and get familiar with basic Django concepts like the request-response cycle, URL routing, and rendering dynamic content.

2. **Building Real-World Applications**: Next, we'll move on to more advanced topics, including working with user authentication, handling forms and file uploads, and creating a blog or e-commerce app.

3. **Advanced Django Features**: The later chapters will introduce more sophisticated topics such as real-time apps with Django Channels, background tasks with Celery, and performance optimization techniques.

4. **Scaling and Maintenance**: We'll conclude the book with best practices for scaling your application, handling traffic spikes, managing versioning and deployments, and ensuring that your application is secure and easy to maintain.

Practical Examples and Exercises

Each chapter includes practical examples, exercises, and real-world scenarios to help you apply what you've learned. By the end of this book, you'll have the skills and confidence to build and deploy sophisticated Django applications that can handle real-world business needs.

Why Django?

Django has become one of the most popular web frameworks for building dynamic and database-driven websites. It's known for its simplicity, flexibility, and scalability, making it an excellent choice for both small projects and large-scale enterprise applications. Django follows the **DRY** (Don't Repeat Yourself) principle, ensuring that your code is concise, efficient, and reusable. With a large community of developers, vast documentation, and numerous third-party packages, Django provides a stable foundation for building web applications of any size.

Django also includes built-in features for handling many common web development tasks, including:

- User authentication and permissions.
- Form handling and validation.
- Robust admin interface for managing data.
- Security features to prevent attacks such as SQL injection, cross-site scripting (XSS), and cross-site request forgery (CSRF).
- Scalable and efficient database management through its ORM.

11

Whether you are building a simple blog, a large e-commerce platform, or a real-time messaging app, Django's rich ecosystem allows you to focus on what matters most: building features and providing value to your users.

Conclusion

Mastering Django: From Basics to Advanced Features is your comprehensive guide to mastering Django and building robust, scalable, and high-performance web applications. Whether you're just starting your web development journey or looking to deepen your understanding of Django, this book will take you through the full process—from building your first Django app to deploying a complex, real-world application.

By the end of this book, you will have the knowledge and skills needed to:

- Build real-world web applications from scratch.
- Work with advanced Django features like Channels, Celery, and asynchronous programming.
- Optimize and scale your Django applications for production.
- Customize Django's admin interface and extend it with third-party libraries and APIs.

- Deploy, maintain, and update your Django applications in a reliable and efficient way.

CHAPTER 1

INTRODUCTION TO WEB DEVELOPMENT WITH PYTHON

The Basics of Web Development

Web development is the process of creating and maintaining websites. It involves everything from building simple static pages to complex web applications. The world of web development is often broken into two main categories:

1. **Frontend Development**: This is everything the user interacts with on a website. It includes the design, structure, and behavior of the website's elements, often using technologies like HTML, CSS, and JavaScript. This part is concerned with the "client-side" of a website.

2. **Backend Development**: This involves the server-side of the application, which handles the logic, database operations, user authentication, and overall functionality of the site. Backend development uses server-side programming languages like Python, PHP, Ruby, and Java.

13

Web development also requires knowledge of **databases**, which store and manage the data your website uses, and **web servers**, which handle requests from users, sending the correct web pages back to them.

Why Python and Django for Building Websites?

Why Python?

Python is an excellent choice for web development for several reasons:

- **Simplicity and Readability**: Python is designed to be easy to read and write, making it an ideal language for developers of all levels. Its syntax is clean, and it follows the principle of "least surprise," meaning the code behaves in an intuitive way.
- **Large Ecosystem**: Python has a massive ecosystem of libraries and frameworks that make it easier to develop web applications. These libraries save time by offering pre-built functionality, meaning developers don't have to reinvent the wheel every time they start a project.
- **Versatility**: Python can be used for a variety of tasks, from data analysis to machine learning, and of course, web development. This versatility means that developers can use Python to build a wide range of applications and tools, even within a web app itself.

- **Growing Community and Support**: Python's large and active community means that help is always just a click away. Whether you're debugging an issue or seeking advice on best practices, there's a huge community of Python developers ready to assist.

Why Django?

Django is a web framework written in Python that simplifies the process of creating complex, database-driven websites. It follows the **Model-Template-View (MTV)** architecture, a variation of the Model-View-Controller (MVC) pattern, making it easy to structure and organize code.

Here's why Django is a great choice for web development:

- **Batteries-Included Approach**: Django comes with many built-in features like user authentication, content administration, site maps, and RSS feeds, which allows developers to focus on building the unique aspects of their applications instead of reinventing basic functionality.
- **Security**: Django is designed with security in mind. It helps developers avoid common security mistakes by providing protections against threats like SQL injection, cross-site scripting, and clickjacking. Its authentication system also ensures that only authorized users can access sensitive parts of the application.

- **Scalability**: Django is highly scalable, allowing developers to build applications that can handle growing amounts of traffic and data. Many large websites and applications use Django because of its ability to scale efficiently.

- **Rapid Development**: With Django's built-in tools, developers can quickly put together a web application. Its structure and modularity allow for faster development, and its emphasis on reusable components and DRY (Don't Repeat Yourself) principles makes code easier to maintain.

- **Rich Documentation**: Django's official documentation is extensive and clear, making it easy for developers to get started and troubleshoot when needed.

Overview of the Web Development Process

Building a website typically involves several stages. The overall web development process can be broken down into the following steps:

1. **Planning and Requirement Gathering**:
   o This stage involves understanding the problem you are trying to solve and the specific requirements for the website. It includes gathering information on user needs, the type of website, and its core functionality.

16

o Questions like: What should the website do? Who is the target audience? What content will the website display? What features are needed?

2. **Design**:

    o The design phase involves creating wireframes and prototypes, which are visual representations of how the site will look and function. This can include user interface (UI) and user experience (UX) design.

    o You will determine layout, color schemes, typography, navigation, and other visual aspects that contribute to the user experience.

3. **Frontend Development**:

    o In this stage, the design is turned into a functional website using **HTML**, **CSS**, and **JavaScript**. These technologies control the layout, styling, and interactive behavior of the site. While Python and Django are used for backend development, frontend languages are responsible for displaying content to the user.

4. **Backend Development**:

    o Here, the server-side logic is developed. This includes creating the models (representing the data structure), handling database operations, and defining how the user will interact with the data. Python and Django come into play here, providing the tools to create dynamic, data-driven websites.

5. **Database Design and Integration**:
   - At this stage, the data structure is built and integrated with the backend. Django's **ORM (Object-Relational Mapping)** system simplifies interactions with databases, making it easier to store and retrieve data.

6. **Testing**:
   - Once the website is built, it needs to be tested to ensure it works as expected. This involves checking for bugs, ensuring compatibility across different browsers and devices, and verifying that the user experience is smooth.

7. **Deployment**:
   - Deployment involves moving the website from a local development environment to a live server so that users can access it. This can include setting up hosting, configuring domain names, and ensuring that the web app is secure and scalable.

8. **Maintenance and Updates**:
   - After deployment, the website needs ongoing maintenance. This includes fixing bugs, adding new features, and ensuring security updates are applied.

This chapter introduces the key concepts of web development and sets the stage for diving deeper into how Python and Django can be used to create dynamic and robust websites. The following chapters will guide readers through the process, providing both foundational knowledge and practical, real-world examples.

CHAPTER 2

SETTING UP YOUR DEVELOPMENT ENVIRONMENT

Installing Python and Django

Before starting web development with Python and Django, you need to set up your development environment. This chapter walks you through the installation process for both Python and Django.

1. Installing Python

Python is the programming language you'll be using to build web applications with Django. To get started, follow these steps to install Python:

- **Step 1: Download Python**
  - Visit the official Python website at https://www.python.org/downloads/.
  - Download the latest stable version of Python for your operating system (Windows, macOS, or Linux).
- **Step 2: Install Python**
  - Run the downloaded installer. On Windows, make sure to check the box labeled "Add Python

to PATH" during installation. This ensures that Python can be accessed from the command line.

- o On macOS and Linux, Python is often pre-installed, but it's good to check the version using the command `python3 --version` or `python --version`.

- **Step 3: Verify Installation**

  - o Open a terminal or command prompt and type the following command:

    ```bash
    ```

    ```
    python --version
    ```

    This should return the version of Python you installed. If you see the version number, Python is installed correctly.

2. Installing Django

Django is a web framework built with Python that simplifies the process of building dynamic websites. To install Django, you'll use Python's package manager, **pip**.

- **Step 1: Install Django via pip**

  - o Open your terminal or command prompt and run the following command:

```
bash

pip install django
```

○ This will download and install Django and its dependencies.

- **Step 2: Verify Django Installation**
  ○ After installation is complete, verify that Django is installed correctly by running:

```
bash

python -m django --version
```

This will return the version of Django that was installed.

Once Python and Django are installed, you're ready to begin building your web applications!

Introduction to Virtual Environments and Dependency Management

As you start developing more complex projects, it's important to manage dependencies (like Django and other libraries). Virtual environments help isolate dependencies for each project, ensuring that different projects don't interfere with each other.

1. What is a Virtual Environment?

A **virtual environment** is an isolated workspace where you can install libraries and dependencies specific to a project without affecting other projects or the global Python environment. It helps you avoid conflicts between different versions of libraries used in different projects.

2. Setting Up a Virtual Environment

To set up a virtual environment for your Django project, follow these steps:

- **Step 1: Install `virtualenv`**
    - o In your terminal or command prompt, install `virtualenv` using pip:

    bash

    ```
    pip install virtualenv
    ```

- **Step 2: Create a Virtual Environment**
    - o Navigate to your project directory and create a new virtual environment:

    bash

    ```
    virtualenv venv
    ```

Here, `venv` is the name of your virtual environment, but you can name it anything you like.

- **Step 3: Activate the Virtual Environment**
  - To activate the virtual environment:
    - On **Windows**, run:

    ```bash
    .\venv\Scripts\activate
    ```

    - On **macOS/Linux**, run:

    ```bash
    source venv/bin/activate
    ```

    - You should now see the name of your virtual environment (`venv`) in your terminal prompt, indicating that it's active.

- **Step 4: Install Django in the Virtual Environment**
  - Now that your virtual environment is active, install Django:

  ```bash
  pip install django
  ```

24

- **Step 5: Deactivate the Virtual Environment**
  - When you're done working, deactivate the virtual environment by running:

```bash
```

```
deactivate
```

This returns you to the global Python environment.

3. Managing Dependencies with `requirements.txt`

To keep track of the libraries and their versions in your project, you can create a `requirements.txt` file. This file is especially helpful when you need to share your project or deploy it on another system.

- **Step 1: Generate `requirements.txt`**
  - After installing all necessary dependencies, run:

```bash
```

```
pip freeze > requirements.txt
```

- **Step 2: Install Dependencies from `requirements.txt`**

- o If someone else is setting up the project or if you're setting it up on a different machine, you can install all dependencies by running:

```bash

pip install -r requirements.txt
```

Choosing a Code Editor and Tools for Web Development

The tools you use to write code are just as important as the programming languages and frameworks. Here are some popular code editors and tools for Python and Django development:

1. Code Editors

A good code editor makes writing and managing code more efficient. Here are some popular options:

- **Visual Studio Code (VS Code)**:
  - o A free, open-source code editor with a wide range of extensions. It's lightweight, fast, and highly customizable. VS Code has excellent Python and Django support, including features like IntelliSense (auto-completion), debugging, and syntax highlighting.
  - o Extensions to install: Python, Django, Pylance, and Python Docstring Generator.
- **PyCharm**:

- o PyCharm is a popular, full-featured Python IDE (Integrated Development Environment) from JetBrains. It has robust support for Django, including Django project templates, debugging tools, and database management.
  - o While PyCharm is a paid tool, the community edition is free and sufficient for most Python and Django development.
- **Sublime Text**:
  - o Sublime Text is a simple and fast code editor with excellent Python syntax highlighting and customizable themes. It also has a package manager to install additional features and plugins.

2. Git for Version Control

Git is essential for version control in web development. It allows you to track changes, collaborate with other developers, and revert to previous versions of your project if something goes wrong.

- **GitHub/GitLab/Bitbucket**:
  - o These are platforms for hosting Git repositories and collaborating on code. GitHub is the most popular, and it integrates with many CI/CD tools and deployment platforms.
  - o Set up a Git repository by running:

```bash
```

```
git init
git add .
git commit -m "Initial commit"
git      remote      add      origin
<repository_url>
git push -u origin master
```

3. Database Management Tools

Django uses databases to store data. For local development, Django's built-in SQLite database is sufficient, but you may need to use more powerful databases like PostgreSQL or MySQL in production. Here are some tools to manage these databases:

- **DBeaver**:
  - A free and open-source database management tool that supports multiple databases, including PostgreSQL, MySQL, and SQLite.
- **pgAdmin** (for PostgreSQL):
  - The official graphical tool for managing PostgreSQL databases. It provides a user-friendly interface to interact with your database, run queries, and manage schemas.

4. Browser Developer Tools

Your web browser's built-in developer tools are essential for testing and debugging your web applications. They allow you to inspect HTML/CSS, monitor network requests, and debug JavaScript.

- Most modern browsers, such as **Google Chrome**, **Firefox**, and **Edge**, come with built-in developer tools. Open them by pressing `F12` or right-clicking on the page and selecting "Inspect."

In this chapter, we've covered the installation of Python and Django, how to create a virtual environment to manage dependencies, and the essential tools for web development. With your environment set up, you can now dive into Django development and start building dynamic web applications!

CHAPTER 3

UNDERSTANDING HTTP AND THE WEB

What is HTTP and How It Works

HTTP (HyperText Transfer Protocol) is the foundation of data communication on the World Wide Web. It is an application-level protocol used to facilitate communication between a **client** (typically a web browser) and a **server** (where a website is hosted).

When you enter a website's URL (Uniform Resource Locator) into your browser's address bar, your browser sends an HTTP request to the server hosting the website. The server then responds with the appropriate data, typically an HTML file, which the browser renders for you to view.

Here's a breakdown of how HTTP works:

1. **Client Requests**:
   - The client (your browser or a web application) sends an HTTP request to a web server. This request includes information such as the URL, the type of request (GET, POST, etc.), and additional headers (like the type of content it can accept).

o For example, when you visit a webpage, the browser sends a **GET** request asking the server to send back the HTML content of the page.

2. **Server Response**:

   o The server processes the client's request and sends back an HTTP response. This response typically includes a **status code** (indicating the result of the request), headers (providing metadata about the response), and the body (the actual data, like HTML, images, or JSON).

   o If the request is successful, the server might send back a **200 OK** status code with the content of the page. If there's an error (e.g., the page is not found), the server might return a **404 Not Found** or a **500 Internal Server Error**.

3. **Stateless Protocol**:

   o HTTP is considered a **stateless protocol**, meaning that each request is independent of the others. Once the server sends a response, it forgets about the request and doesn't retain any information for the next one. If you need to maintain information across multiple requests (such as logging in to a website), this is achieved through **cookies** or **sessions**.

4. **Methods (HTTP Verbs)**:

o **GET**: Requests data from the server (e.g., when you load a webpage).

o **POST**: Sends data to the server, often used when submitting forms (e.g., creating an account or posting a comment).

o **PUT**: Replaces existing data on the server (e.g., updating a profile).

o **DELETE**: Removes data from the server (e.g., deleting a post).

o **PATCH**: Partially updates data on the server.

5. **Status Codes**:

o Status codes in the response are divided into categories based on their meaning:

- **1xx**: Informational responses (e.g., "100 Continue").

- **2xx**: Success responses (e.g., "200 OK").

- **3xx**: Redirection (e.g., "301 Moved Permanently").

- **4xx**: Client errors (e.g., "404 Not Found").

- **5xx**: Server errors (e.g., "500 Internal Server Error").

Client-Server Model

The **client-server model** is a fundamental concept in web development and networking. It's a way of structuring the interaction between devices or programs that request and provide services over a network. This model separates the roles of the client (the requestor) and the server (the provider).

1. Client:

- A client is a device or application that makes a request to a server. It can be a web browser, mobile app, or any other program capable of sending HTTP requests to a server.
- For example, when you open a browser and type in a URL, the browser acts as a client and sends an HTTP request to the server hosting that website.

2. Server:

- A server is a machine or application that waits for incoming requests from clients and responds with the appropriate data. The server hosts the website or web application and handles tasks like data processing, managing databases, and serving static files (e.g., images, CSS, JavaScript).
- When a server receives an HTTP request, it processes it and sends back an HTTP response containing the requested information.

3. Communication:

- The communication between the client and the server is usually **request-response**. The client makes a request, and the server processes it and sends back a response. This is often done over a **TCP/IP** connection.
- The request might include various details, such as query parameters (e.g., `?user=john`), cookies (for session management), headers (for content-type and language preferences), and the body (for POST requests).

4. Example:

- Imagine you're browsing an online store. When you search for a product, your web browser (client) sends an HTTP GET request to the server, asking for a list of products matching your search criteria. The server responds by sending back an HTML page with the product listings, which the browser then displays to you.

Basic Web Protocols and Concepts

In addition to HTTP, several other web protocols and concepts are key to understanding how the web works. These protocols ensure communication between clients and servers and help deliver content efficiently.

1. DNS (Domain Name System):

- DNS is like the "phonebook" of the internet. It translates human-readable domain names (like `www.example.com`) into IP addresses (e.g., `192.0.2.1`), which computers use to locate each other on the internet. When you type a website URL into your browser, your browser queries DNS to find the correct IP address of the server hosting that site.

2. HTTPS (HyperText Transfer Protocol Secure):

- HTTPS is the secure version of HTTP. It uses **SSL/TLS encryption** to protect data between the client and the server. It's used to ensure privacy and data integrity, particularly for sensitive information like passwords, credit card numbers, and personal details.
- When a URL starts with `https://` rather than `http://`, it means the connection is encrypted using HTTPS.

3. TCP/IP (Transmission Control Protocol/Internet Protocol):

- TCP/IP is a set of protocols that govern how data is transmitted over the internet. It ensures that data sent from the client reaches the server and that the server's response is delivered back to the client correctly.
- HTTP operates on top of TCP/IP, meaning that HTTP requests and responses are carried over TCP/IP connections.

4. Cookies:

- Cookies are small pieces of data stored by the client (usually in the web browser) that are sent with HTTP requests to the server. They are commonly used for maintaining state in stateless protocols like HTTP. For example, cookies are used to remember login sessions or store user preferences.

- A server might set a cookie by including a `Set-Cookie` header in the HTTP response, and the client sends the cookie back with subsequent requests in the `Cookie` header.

5. Caching:

- Caching is a technique used to store copies of frequently requested resources (like images, web pages, or API responses) so that they can be quickly retrieved without re-requesting them from the server. This speeds up loading times and reduces server load.

- Web browsers and servers can use caching headers, such as `Cache-Control` and `ETag`, to manage how resources are cached.

6. WebSockets:

- WebSockets provide a full-duplex communication channel over a single TCP connection. Unlike HTTP, which follows a request-response model, WebSockets allow for continuous, real-time communication between the client and server.

- WebSockets are often used in applications that require real-time data updates, such as live chats, stock market updates, or multiplayer games.

7. REST (Representational State Transfer):

- REST is an architectural style for building web services. It is based on HTTP and uses standard HTTP methods (GET, POST, PUT, DELETE) to perform CRUD (Create, Read, Update, Delete) operations on resources. RESTful APIs are commonly used in web applications to allow different systems to communicate with each other.

By understanding HTTP, the client-server model, and essential web protocols, you're now equipped with the foundational knowledge required to begin developing dynamic websites and web applications. These concepts are critical to understanding how data flows across the web and how client-side and server-side components interact to deliver content. The following chapters will build on this foundation, focusing on how to use Python and Django to bring this all together in a web development project.

CHAPTER 4

INTRODUCTION TO DJANGO FRAMEWORK

What is Django?

Django is a high-level, open-source web framework for Python that enables rapid development of secure and maintainable websites. It was designed to simplify the process of building complex web applications by providing a set of pre-built tools and libraries for common web development tasks, such as handling requests, interacting with databases, and rendering templates.

Django follows the **Model-Template-View (MTV)** architecture, a variation of the **Model-View-Controller (MVC)** pattern. This architecture helps organize code into distinct layers, making it easier to maintain and scale web applications.

Key Features of Django:

- **Batteries-included**: Django comes with many built-in features that are essential for web development, such as user authentication, URL routing, form handling, and a powerful admin interface.

- **Scalability and Reusability**: Django's modular design encourages code reusability, making it easy to scale applications as they grow.
- **Security**: Django emphasizes security, offering built-in protections against common threats like SQL injection, cross-site scripting (XSS), and cross-site request forgery (CSRF).

History of Django and Its Advantages

History of Django:

Django was created by **Adrian Holovaty** and **Simon Willison** in 2003 as part of a project for a newspaper called the Lawrence Journal-World in Kansas, USA. They were tasked with building web applications for journalists to manage and display news content. The framework was originally built to help developers quickly build news sites with dynamic content management, but over time, it was developed into a full-fledged web framework for general-purpose web applications.

In 2005, Django was released as open-source software under the BSD license, allowing developers from around the world to contribute to the framework's growth. Since then, Django has become one of the most popular web frameworks in the Python ecosystem.

Advantages of Django:

1. **Rapid Development**: Django's "batteries-included" philosophy and high-level abstractions allow developers to create web applications quickly. Many of the tasks that typically require significant development effort (like user authentication, database models, and administrative interfaces) are already built into Django.

2. **Scalability**: Django is highly scalable, which makes it suitable for building everything from small applications to large, high-traffic sites. Many companies and platforms like Instagram, Pinterest, and Disqus use Django because of its scalability.

3. **Security**: Django provides built-in protections against many common security vulnerabilities. For instance, it handles user authentication, stores passwords securely, and protects against SQL injection, cross-site scripting, and cross-site request forgery.

4. **Reusability**: Django promotes reusable code, which helps avoid duplication and allows developers to build modular applications. It encourages you to write clean, maintainable code that can be easily reused across multiple projects.

5. **Large and Active Community**: Django has a large and vibrant community of developers who contribute to the framework's growth. This means there's a wealth of tutorials, plugins, and support available, making it easier for developers to learn and use Django.

6. **Strong Documentation**: Django's official documentation is one of its strongest assets. It provides clear, in-depth explanations and examples, helping both beginners and experts understand how to use the framework effectively.

Key Features of Django

Django's core features are designed to help developers streamline the web development process, ensuring that building secure and scalable web applications is both efficient and straightforward. Below are the key features of Django:

1. **MTV Architecture**:
   o **Model-Template-View (MTV)** is Django's variant of the popular **Model-View-Controller (MVC)** pattern. It helps organize the web application into three main components:
      ▪ **Model**: This is the layer where the data is stored. It defines the structure of your database, typically using Django's **Object-Relational Mapping (ORM)**. Models represent database tables and provide an interface for querying and updating data.
      ▪ **Template**: Templates handle the presentation layer of your application. They define how the data is displayed to

41

users (e.g., HTML files). Django uses its own template language to dynamically generate HTML content.

- **View**: Views handle the business logic of the application. They receive requests, process them (often by querying the model), and return the appropriate response, usually in the form of an HTTP response.

2. **Object-Relational Mapping (ORM)**:

   o Django's ORM allows developers to interact with the database using Python code rather than raw SQL queries. This provides an abstraction layer that simplifies database operations.

   o You define database models as Python classes, and Django automatically converts them into SQL tables. For example:

```python
python

class Book(models.Model):
    title                = models.CharField(max_length=100)
    author               = models.CharField(max_length=100)
    published_date       = models.DateField()
```

Django then provides an easy-to-use API to query the database and manage data, such as:

```python
books                          =
Book.objects.filter(author="J.K.
Rowling")
```

3. **URL Routing**:

   o Django uses a powerful URL dispatcher that allows developers to map URLs to specific views. This makes it easy to define how URLs are handled and which views should be triggered for different paths.

   o For example, you can map a URL like `/books/` to a specific view that retrieves a list of books from the database and displays them:

```python
from django.urls import path
from . import views

urlpatterns = [
    path('books/', views.book_list),
]
```

4. **Admin Interface**:

- One of Django's standout features is its automatically generated admin interface. When you define your models, Django can create a powerful admin panel that allows you to manage the data directly from a web interface.
- This means that, for example, if you have a model for `Book`, Django will automatically generate an interface for adding, editing, and deleting books without you needing to write any additional code.

5. **Authentication and Authorization**:

- Django comes with built-in authentication features, including user login, logout, and password management. It also supports user roles and permissions, so you can easily control who can access different parts of your application.
- For instance, you can limit access to certain views only to authenticated users or users with specific roles.

6. **Forms**:

- Django simplifies the handling of forms (for example, user registration or contact forms). It provides tools for rendering forms, validating user input, and processing the data. Django can even generate forms directly from models, reducing the need to write repetitive code.

- o Django forms also provide built-in security features, such as protection against cross-site request forgery (CSRF) attacks.

7. **Security Features**:
   - o Django is designed with security in mind. It includes protections against many common security threats:
     - **SQL Injection**: Django's ORM automatically escapes SQL queries, preventing SQL injection attacks.
     - **Cross-Site Scripting (XSS)**: Django automatically escapes user-generated content in templates, preventing XSS attacks.
     - **Cross-Site Request Forgery (CSRF)**: Django includes a middleware that protects against CSRF attacks, ensuring that requests made to the server are from trusted sources.
     - **Clickjacking Protection**: Django includes middleware that prevents the site from being embedded in iframes, mitigating clickjacking attacks.

8. **Internationalization and Localization**:
   - o Django makes it easy to build applications that can be used in different languages and regions. It

includes support for translating text, formatting dates and numbers, and handling various locale-specific content.

o   This makes it simple to expand your application to a global audience.

9. **Caching**:

o   Django supports caching mechanisms that can significantly improve the performance of your application. It can cache database queries, views, and static files, reducing the load on your server and speeding up page rendering.

10. **Testing Framework**:

o   Django comes with a built-in testing framework that allows developers to write unit tests for their application's models, views, and templates. This helps ensure that your application behaves correctly and reduces the likelihood of bugs.

Summary

Django is a powerful web framework that simplifies the process of building dynamic and secure websites. It follows the **MTV architecture**, making it easy to organize code and maintain a clean structure. Django's **ORM** allows you to interact with databases using Python, eliminating the need for writing complex SQL queries. The built-in **admin interface**, **authentication system**, and **security features** make it easy to build robust web applications that are secure, scalable, and maintainable. Whether you're building a small blog or a large-scale web application, Django offers a comprehensive set of tools to help you get the job done efficiently.

CHAPTER 5

CREATING YOUR FIRST DJANGO PROJECT

Setting Up a New Django Project

Now that you have Django installed and your environment set up, it's time to create your first Django project. A **Django project** is a collection of settings, configurations, and files that work together to form a web application.

Step 1: Create a New Django Project

1. Open your terminal or command prompt.
2. Navigate to the directory where you want to create your project. You can use the `cd` command to change directories.
3. Run the following command to create a new Django project:

```
bash
```

```
django-admin startproject myproject
```

Replace `myproject` with whatever you want to name your project.

Step 2: Navigate to the Project Directory

Once the project is created, navigate to the project folder:

```
bash
```

```
cd myproject
```

This will take you into the root directory of your new Django project.

Understanding the Folder Structure

After running the `startproject` command, Django creates several files and folders for you. Let's go over what each of these is and what role it plays in your project.

Here's the folder structure for a typical Django project:

```
markdown
```

```
myproject/
    manage.py
    myproject/
        __init__.py
        settings.py
        urls.py
        asgi.py
        wsgi.py
```

1. **manage.py**:

   o This is a command-line utility that helps manage various tasks in your Django project. You'll use it to run the development server, create databases, and manage other administrative tasks. For example, you can run the development server with:

   ```
   bash
   ```

   ```
   python manage.py runserver
   ```

2. **The Inner myproject/ Directory**:

   o This is the main package for your project. It contains several important files:

   ▪ **__init__.py**: This file indicates that this directory is a Python package. It's necessary for Python to recognize it as a module.

   ▪ **settings.py**: This file contains all of the project's settings, such as database configurations, installed apps, middleware, and static file settings. It's one of the most important files in any Django project.

   ▪ **urls.py**: This file contains the URL routing for your project. It maps URLs to views. You'll add URL patterns here to define how different requests are handled.

- **`asgi.py` and `wsgi.py`**: These files are responsible for providing an entry point to your application for different web servers. `wsgi.py` is used for synchronous applications, while `asgi.py` is used for asynchronous applications.

Running the Development Server and Viewing Your First Page

Step 1: Run the Development Server

With your project set up, the next step is to run the Django development server and view your first page.

1. In the terminal, while in your project directory, run the following command:

```bash
```

```
python manage.py runserver
```

This starts the development server on your local machine, typically at `http://127.0.0.1:8000/` (localhost on port 8000).

51

2. Open a web browser and go to `http://127.0.0.1:8000/`. You should see Django's default welcome page, which indicates that your project has been successfully set up and the server is running.

Step 2: Exploring the Default Welcome Page

The default Django welcome page provides a few useful links, such as:

- Links to documentation and tutorials to help you get started.
- A link to the Django admin interface (which we will cover in later chapters).
- A link to the settings page where you can manage the project.

Customizing the Project

Now that you have your first Django project running, let's take a closer look at the next steps you might take as you start building your application.

Step 1: Create Your First App

Django projects are composed of **apps**, which are individual modules of your project that handle specific functionality. For example, you might have an app for handling user authentication, another for blog posts, or one for managing products in an online store.

To create a new app, follow these steps:

1. In the project's root directory, run:

```bash
python manage.py startapp myapp
```

Replace `myapp` with the name of your app. This will create a new folder named `myapp` inside the project directory with the following structure:

```markdown
myapp/
    migrations/
    __init__.py
    admin.py
    apps.py
    models.py
    tests.py
    views.py
```

2. Register the app in `settings.py`:
    o Open the `settings.py` file in the `myproject/myproject/` directory.

o Find the `INSTALLED_APPS` list and add the name of your app to it:

```python
INSTALLED_APPS = [
    # other apps
    'myapp',
]
```

Step 2: Create Your First View

Now that we have an app, we can create a simple view to render a page.

1. In the `myapp/views.py` file, add a view function:

```python
from django.http import HttpResponse

def home(request):
    return HttpResponse("Hello, welcome to my Django app!")
```

Step 3: Map the View to a URL

Next, we'll map the view to a URL so that we can access it in a web browser.

1. Create a `urls.py` file in the `myapp` directory (if it doesn't already exist).

2. In `myapp/urls.py`, add the following code:

python

```python
from django.urls import path
from . import views

urlpatterns = [
    path('', views.home, name='home'),
]
```

3. In the `myproject/urls.py` file (the one in the project's main directory), include the `myapp` URLs by adding the following import at the top:

python

```python
from django.urls import include, path
```

Then, in the `urlpatterns` list, add:

python

```python
urlpatterns = [
    path('', include('myapp.urls')),
]
```

Step 4: Refresh and View Your Page

Now that we've mapped the `home` view to the root URL (`/`), run the server again:

```
bash
```

```
python manage.py runserver
```

Navigate to `http://127.0.0.1:8000/` in your browser. You should see the message "Hello, welcome to my Django app!" displayed on the page.

Summary

In this chapter, you've learned how to create a new Django project, understand its folder structure, and run the development server to view the default welcome page. You also created your first app, added a simple view, and mapped it to a URL to display content. These are the basic steps involved in starting any Django project, and as you continue, you'll build on this foundation to create more complex and dynamic web applications.

CHAPTER 6

DJANGO MODELS –
INTRODUCTION TO DATABASES

What Are Models in Django?

In Django, **models** are Python classes that define the structure of your database. Each model class represents a table in the database, and each instance of the class represents a record (or row) in that table. Models allow you to interact with your database in an object-oriented way, without needing to write raw SQL queries.

For example, imagine you're building a blog application. You could define a `Post` model to represent blog posts. Each blog post would have fields like a title, content, and publish date. Django uses models to automatically generate the SQL needed to create and interact with this table.

Example of a Simple Django Model:

python

```
from django.db import models

class Post(models.Model):
    title = models.CharField(max_length=100)
```

```
content = models.TextField()
published_date                          =
models.DateTimeField(auto_now_add=True)

def __str__(self):
    return self.title
```

In this example:

- The `Post` class is a model that represents a blog post.
- The `title`, `content`, and `published_date` fields correspond to columns in the database table for the `Post` model.
- `CharField` and `TextField` are field types provided by Django to store text data.
- `DateTimeField` is used for date and time data.
- The `__str__` method is defined to return the title of the post when an instance is printed.

Introduction to ORM (Object-Relational Mapping)

Django's **Object-Relational Mapping (ORM)** system allows you to work with your database using Python code instead of writing raw SQL queries. The ORM automatically converts your Python objects (like the `Post` model) into SQL statements and vice versa.

Here's how ORM helps:

- **Database Abstraction**: You can interact with your database using Python objects. This means you don't have to worry about SQL syntax. Django handles all the database interactions behind the scenes.
- **Portability**: Django's ORM allows your code to work with multiple database backends (such as PostgreSQL, MySQL, SQLite, etc.) without changing the code that interacts with the database. You only need to configure your database settings in `settings.py`.
- **Query Building**: The ORM allows you to build complex queries using Python code, which Django then converts into SQL.

Basic Operations with Django ORM:

1. **Creating a Model Instance**: You can create a new record in the database by creating an instance of a model and saving it.

```python
python

post = Post(title="First Blog Post",
content="This is the content of the blog
post.")
post.save()     # Save the post to the
database
```

2. **Querying the Database**: You can query the database for records using the model's `objects` attribute.

   o **Getting all records**:

   ```python
   all_posts = Post.objects.all()
   ```

   o **Filtering records**:

   ```python
   recent_posts = Post.objects.filter(published_date_year=2022)
   ```

   o **Getting a single record**:

   ```python
   first_post = Post.objects.get(id=1)
   ```

3. **Updating Records**: You can update records by modifying the instance and calling `save()`.

   ```python
   post = Post.objects.get(id=1)
   post.title = "Updated Blog Post Title"
   post.save()
   ```

60

4. **Deleting Records**: You can delete records from the database using the `delete()` method.

```python
python

post = Post.objects.get(id=1)
post.delete()
```

5. **Ordering Records**: You can order query results using the `order_by()` method.

```python
python

ordered_posts                          =
Post.objects.all().order_by('-
published_date')  # Descending order
```

Creating and Managing Database Models

Now that you understand what Django models are and how the ORM works, let's walk through the process of creating and managing database models in Django.

Step 1: Define Your Model

To define a model, you need to subclass Django's `models.Model` class and define fields as class attributes. Each field corresponds to a column in the database table.

Example of a model definition:

```python
python

from django.db import models

class Author(models.Model):
    name = models.CharField(max_length=100)
    bio = models.TextField()
    birth_date = models.DateField()

    def __str__(self):
        return self.name
```

This model represents an `Author` with a name, biography, and birth date. Each field has a specific type that Django uses to map it to the correct column type in the database.

Step 2: Run Migrations

Once you've defined your model, Django needs to create the corresponding database table. Django uses **migrations** to track changes to your models and apply them to the database.

1. First, create a migration by running the following command:

```bash
bash

python manage.py makemigrations
```

This command looks for any changes in your models and creates a migration file to apply those changes.

2. Next, apply the migration to the database:

```bash
```

```
python manage.py migrate
```

This command creates the actual database tables based on your models. It reads the migration files and executes the necessary SQL commands to update the database schema.

Step 3: Interacting with the Model via the Django Shell

You can interact with your models directly using the Django shell. This is useful for testing or exploring your database.

To enter the Django shell, run:

```bash
```

```
python manage.py shell
```

Once inside the shell, you can create, query, and modify model instances. For example:

```python
```

```
from myapp.models import Author
```

63

```
author = Author(name="Jane Doe", bio="A well-
known author", birth_date="1980-05-15")
author.save()


# Querying the database
authors = Author.objects.all()
```

Step 4: Using Django Admin to Manage Models

Django comes with a built-in **admin interface** that allows you to manage your models through a web interface. To make a model accessible in the admin panel:

1. Open the `myapp/admin.py` file and register the model:

   ```python
   python
   ```

   ```python
   from django.contrib import admin
   from .models import Author

   admin.site.register(Author)
   ```

2. To use the admin interface, you need to create a superuser (an admin account). Run:

   ```bash
   bash
   ```

   ```bash
   python manage.py createsuperuser
   ```

Follow the prompts to create a username, email, and password for the superuser.

3. Once the superuser is created, run the development server:

```bash
```

```
python manage.py runserver
```

Visit `http://127.0.0.1:8000/admin` in your browser, log in with your superuser credentials, and you'll be able to manage the `Author` model (and any other models you register) through the admin interface.

Summary

In this chapter, we learned about Django models and their role in representing database tables. We covered the basics of **Object-Relational Mapping (ORM)** and how Django's ORM abstracts database operations into Python code, making it easier to interact with databases. We also walked through the steps to create, manage, and query database models, including using migrations to update the database schema, interacting with models through the Django shell, and managing models via the Django admin interface.

As you build your Django applications, models will be the foundation of your database structure and interactions.

Understanding how to define and manage models efficiently is key to building robust and scalable web applications.

CHAPTER 7

WORKING WITH COLLECTIONS IN KOTLIN

Kotlin provides powerful and flexible ways to handle collections of data. Collections are an essential part of most applications as they allow you to store, manipulate, and process groups of objects. In this chapter, we'll explore Kotlin's main collection types— **Lists**, **Sets**, and **Maps**—as well as techniques for iterating, filtering, transforming, and sorting data. We'll also look at how Kotlin handles **nullability** in collections.

Lists, Sets, and Maps

1. Lists

A **List** in Kotlin is an ordered collection that allows duplicates. It is a collection of elements that maintains the order in which they are added. Kotlin has two types of lists:

- **MutableList**: A list that allows modification (adding, removing, or updating elements).
- **List**: An immutable list, which cannot be changed after its creation.

Creating a List:

- **Immutable List:**

```kotlin
val numbers = listOf(1, 2, 3, 4, 5)
```

- **Mutable List:**

```kotlin
val mutableNumbers = mutableListOf(1, 2, 3,
4, 5)
mutableNumbers.add(6)
```

You can access elements by index:

```kotlin
val firstElement = numbers[0]  // Accessing the
first element
```

2. Sets

A **Set** is an unordered collection of unique elements. It does not allow duplicates, meaning that if you attempt to add an element that is already present, it won't be added again. Kotlin also provides mutable and immutable sets:

- **Immutable Set:**

```kotlin
kotlin
```

```kotlin
val uniqueNumbers = setOf(1, 2, 3, 4, 5)
```

- **Mutable Set:**

```kotlin
kotlin
```

```kotlin
val mutableUniqueNumbers = mutableSetOf(1,
2, 3, 4, 5)
mutableUniqueNumbers.add(6)
```

3. Maps

A **Map** is a collection of key-value pairs, where each key is unique, and each key maps to exactly one value. Kotlin provides two types of maps:

- **MutableMap**: A map where you can modify the entries (add or remove key-value pairs).
- **Map**: An immutable map that cannot be modified.

Creating a Map:

- **Immutable Map:**

```kotlin
kotlin
```

```
val capitals = mapOf("USA" to "Washington
D.C.", "France" to "Paris")
```

- **Mutable Map:**

```kotlin
val mutableCapitals = mutableMapOf("USA"
to "Washington D.C.", "France" to "Paris")
mutableCapitals["Germany"] = "Berlin"  //
Adding a new key-value pair
```

You can access values by key:

```kotlin
val capitalOfFrance = capitals["France"]
```

Iterating Over Collections

Kotlin makes it easy to iterate over collections, and there are several methods to do so, whether you're working with lists, sets, or maps.

1. Iterating Over a List:

You can iterate over a list using loops or higher-order functions like `forEach`:

- **Using a `for` loop:**

```kotlin
val numbers = listOf(1, 2, 3, 4, 5)
for (number in numbers) {
    println(number)
}
```

- **Using `forEach`:**

```kotlin
numbers.forEach { number ->
    println(number)
}
```

2. Iterating Over a Set:

Since sets are unordered, iteration doesn't guarantee any specific order:

```kotlin
val uniqueNumbers = setOf(1, 2, 3, 4, 5)
uniqueNumbers.forEach { number ->
    println(number)
}
```

3. Iterating Over a Map:

You can iterate over a map's entries (key-value pairs) using a `for` loop or `forEach`:

- **Using a `for` loop**:

```kotlin
val capitals = mapOf("USA" to "Washington
D.C.", "France" to "Paris")
for ((country, capital) in capitals) {
    println("$country: $capital")
}
```

- **Using `forEach`**:

```kotlin
capitals.forEach { (country, capital) ->
    println("$country: $capital")
}
```

Filtering, Transforming, and Sorting Data

Kotlin provides a wide array of functions that allow you to filter, transform, and sort data in your collections.

1. Filtering Data

You can use the `filter` function to create a new collection containing only the elements that match a certain condition.

72

- **Example of filtering a list of numbers**:

```kotlin
val numbers = listOf(1, 2, 3, 4, 5, 6)
val evenNumbers = numbers.filter { it % 2
== 0 }
println(evenNumbers)  // Output: [2, 4, 6]
```

2. Transforming Data

Kotlin allows you to transform collections using functions like map and flatMap. The map function transforms each element of the collection based on a provided transformation function.

- **Example of transforming a list of numbers into their squares**:

```kotlin
val numbers = listOf(1, 2, 3, 4, 5)
val squaredNumbers = numbers.map { it * it
}
println(squaredNumbers)  // Output: [1, 4,
9, 16, 25]
```

3. Sorting Data

You can use the `sorted` function to sort a collection in ascending order, and `sortedDescending` for descending order. Both functions return a new sorted list.

- **Sorting a list of numbers**:

  ```kotlin
  val numbers = listOf(5, 3, 1, 4, 2)
  val sortedNumbers = numbers.sorted()
  println(sortedNumbers)  // Output: [1, 2, 3, 4, 5]
  ```

- **Sorting in descending order**:

  ```kotlin
  val sortedDescendingNumbers = numbers.sortedDescending()
  println(sortedDescendingNumbers)  // Output: [5, 4, 3, 2, 1]
  ```

4. Combining Filter, Map, and Sort

You can chain operations to filter, transform, and sort data in a single line:

```kotlin
val numbers = listOf(1, 2, 3, 4, 5, 6)
```

74

```
val result = numbers.filter { it % 2 == 0 }   //
Filter even numbers
                    .map { it * it }           //
Square the even numbers
                    .sortedDescending()        //
Sort in descending order
println(result)  // Output: [36, 16, 4]
```

Handling Nullability with Collections

Kotlin has built-in null safety features that help prevent null pointer exceptions. Collections can contain nullable elements, and Kotlin provides various tools to handle them safely.

1. Nullable Types in Collections

You can define collections that hold nullable elements by using the ? syntax.

- **Example of a list containing nullable elements**:

  ```
  kotlin
  ```

  ```
  val    nullableList:    List<String?>    =
  listOf("apple", null, "banana", null)
  ```

2. Handling Nullability with Safe Calls

Kotlin provides safe calls (?.) to prevent exceptions when dealing with nullable values.

- **Example of using safe calls**:

```kotlin
val    nullableList:    List<String?>    =
listOf("apple", null, "banana")
val              firstNonNull              =
nullableList.firstOrNull {  it  !=  null
}?.toUpperCase()
println(firstNonNull)  // Output: "APPLE"
```

3. Filtering Out Null Values

You can use the `filterNotNull()` function to create a new collection that excludes null values.

- **Example**:

```kotlin
val    nullableList:    List<String?>    =
listOf("apple", null, "banana")
val              nonNullList              =
nullableList.filterNotNull()
println(nonNullList)  // Output: [apple,
banana]
```

4. Handling Null in Maps

If you want to handle potential null values when accessing elements in a map, you can use the safe call operator or getOrDefault().

- **Example using safe calls**:

```kotlin
val map = mapOf("A" to "Apple", "B" to "Banana")
val value = map["C"]?.toUpperCase()   // Will return null as "C" does not exist
println(value)  // Output: null
```

- **Example using getOrDefault()**:

```kotlin
val valueOrDefault = map.getOrDefault("C", "Default Value")
println(valueOrDefault)        // Output: Default Value
```

Summary

In this chapter, we explored Kotlin's collections: **Lists**, **Sets**, and **Maps**. We learned how to create, access, and modify collections, as well as how to iterate over them using different methods. Kotlin's higher-order functions, like `filter`, `map`, and `sorted`, provide powerful ways to process and transform data in collections. Additionally, we saw how to handle nullability in collections using Kotlin's safe calls, `filterNotNull()`, and `getOrDefault()` to avoid null pointer exceptions and ensure safer code.

Understanding how to work with collections is fundamental to mastering Kotlin and efficiently processing data in your applications.

CHAPTER 8

DJANGO TEMPLATES – BUILDING DYNAMIC WEB PAGES

Django templates are used to create dynamic HTML pages by embedding Python-like logic into HTML files. They allow you to separate the content, structure, and presentation of your web pages. In this chapter, we'll explore the basics of Django templates, how to use template tags and filters, and how to render dynamic data within templates.

Introduction to Django Templates

A **Django template** is an HTML file that contains special syntax to dynamically generate content. The template allows you to insert dynamic data from the backend (like database records or user input) and render it on a web page. This is done through Django's templating engine, which uses a combination of **template tags**, **filters**, and **variables** to generate the final HTML.

A basic Django template looks like a regular HTML file, but it contains placeholders for dynamic data. For example, you might have a template for displaying a list of blog posts where each post's title and content are rendered from the database.

Example of a Simple Template:

```
html
```

```
<!DOCTYPE html>
<html>
<head>
    <title>My Blog</title>
</head>
<body>
    <h1>{{ post.title }}</h1>
    <p>{{ post.content }}</p>
</body>
</html>
```

In this template:

- `{{ post.title }}` and `{{ post.content }}` are placeholders for dynamic data that will be filled in when the template is rendered by the server.

Django's templating engine provides a powerful way to insert dynamic data and control the flow of content in your HTML files.

Using Template Tags and Filters

Django templates use **template tags** and **filters** to manipulate data and control the structure of the rendered HTML. Template tags are enclosed in `{% %}`, while variables are enclosed in `{{ }}`.

1. Template Tags

Template tags are used to perform logic within the template. Some of the most common template tags are:

- `{% for %}`: Loops over a list of items.
- `{% if %}`: Conditional logic for rendering content based on certain conditions.
- `{% include %}`: Includes another template within the current template.
- `{% block %}`: Used for template inheritance to define content blocks.

Example of using `{% for %}` to loop through a list of posts:

html

```
<!DOCTYPE html>
<html>
<head>
    <title>My Blog</title>
</head>
<body>
    <h1>Recent Posts</h1>
    <ul>
        {% for post in posts %}
            <li>{{ post.title }}</li>
        {% empty %}
            <li>No posts available</li>
```

81

```
        {% endfor %}
    </ul>
</body>
</html>
```

In this example:

- {% for post in posts %} loops through all posts and renders their titles inside <li> elements.
- {% empty %} is an optional tag that renders a message when the list is empty.

2. Template Filters

Filters are used to modify the value of a variable before rendering it. They are applied using the pipe (|) symbol.

Some common template filters include:

- **date**: Formats a date.
- **length**: Returns the length of a list or string.
- **default**: Provides a default value if the variable is empty or undefined.
- **lower**: Converts a string to lowercase.

Example of using filters:

```
html
```

82

```
<p>Published on: {{ post.published_date|date:"F
j, Y" }}</p>
<p>Number of characters in the title: {{
post.title|length }}</p>
```

In this example:

- `{{ post.published_date|date:"F j, Y" }}` formats the date of the post into a readable format like "March 10, 2025".
- `{{ post.title|length }}` returns the number of characters in the post's title.

Rendering Dynamic Data in Templates

Django templates are powerful tools for rendering dynamic content on your web pages. They allow you to pass data from the views to the templates and dynamically update the content based on user actions or database entries.

1. Passing Data to Templates

When rendering a template in Django, you can pass dynamic data from the view to the template by using the **context** dictionary. The context contains key-value pairs, where the keys are the variable names that can be used in the template, and the values are the data you want to display.

Example of passing data from a view to a template:

- In the `views.py` file:

python

```python
from django.shortcuts import render
from .models import Post

def post_list(request):
    posts = Post.objects.all()
    return render(request, 'post_list.html',
{'posts': posts})
```

In this view:

- We query the `Post` model to get all the posts.
- We pass the `posts` variable to the template `post_list.html` through the context dictionary.
- In the `post_list.html` template:

html

```html
<!DOCTYPE html>
<html>
<head>
    <title>My Blog</title>
</head>
<body>
    <h1>Recent Posts</h1>
    <ul>
```

84

```
        {% for post in posts %}
            <li>{{ post.title }}</li>
        {% empty %}
            <li>No posts available</li>
        {% endfor %}
    </ul>
</body>
</html>
```

Here, the template will display the titles of all the posts passed from the view.

2. Dynamic Content with Conditionals

You can render different content depending on certain conditions using {% if %} tags. This allows for more dynamic web pages where content can change based on logic.

Example of using {% if %} for conditionals:

html

```
<h1>Welcome, {{ user.username }}!</h1>

{% if user.is_authenticated %}
    <p>You are logged in</p>
{% else %}
    <p>Please log in to access your account.</p>
{% endif %}
```

In this example:

- The `{% if user.is_authenticated %}` tag checks if the user is logged in, and displays a different message based on the result.

3. Template Inheritance

One of the most powerful features of Django templates is template inheritance. This allows you to create a base template with common structure (like headers, footers, and navigation) and extend it in other templates to avoid code duplication.

Example of a base template (`base.html`):

```html
html

<!DOCTYPE html>
<html>
<head>
    <title>{% block title %}My Blog{% endblock %}</title>
</head>
<body>
    <header>
        <h1>Welcome to My Blog</h1>
    </header>

    <div>
```

```
    {% block content %}
    <!-- Content will go here -->
    {% endblock %}
</div>

<footer>
    <p>My Blog &; 2025</p>
</footer>
</body>
</html>
```

In this base template:

- {% block title %} and {% block content %} are placeholder blocks where child templates can insert content.

Example of a child template (`post_list.html`):

html

```
{% extends 'base.html' %}

{% block title %}Post List{% endblock %}

{% block content %}
    <h2>Recent Posts</h2>
    <ul>
        {% for post in posts %}
            <li>{{ post.title }}</li>
```

87

```
        {% empty %}
            <li>No posts available</li>
        {% endfor %}
    </ul>
{% endblock %}
```

In this child template:

- `{% extends 'base.html' %}` tells Django to extend the `base.html` template.
- `{% block content %}` defines the content section of the page, which will replace the corresponding block in `base.html`.

Summary

In this chapter, we've covered the basics of **Django templates** and how they help you build dynamic web pages. We explored the use of **template tags** for looping through lists and applying conditional logic, as well as **template filters** for transforming data before rendering it. Additionally, we looked at how to render dynamic data in templates by passing context from views, using **template inheritance** to avoid code duplication, and dynamically displaying content based on conditions.

By mastering Django templates, you can separate your application's logic from its presentation, making your web pages more flexible and easier to maintain. As you move forward, you'll build on this foundation to create fully dynamic and interactive websites with Django.

CHAPTER 9

DJANGO FORMS – HANDLING USER INPUT

Handling user input is a critical aspect of web development, and Django provides an easy-to-use framework for working with forms. In this chapter, we'll explore how Django forms work, how to create forms for handling user input, and how to validate and save form data efficiently.

Introduction to Forms in Django

In Django, forms are used to collect data from users and validate that the data meets certain requirements before processing it. Django offers both **Django Forms** and **ModelForms** for this purpose. The difference between them is that Django Forms are more generic and can be used for any kind of input, whereas ModelForms are specifically tied to Django models and are used for data related to models.

A Django form contains several components:

1. **Form Fields**: These define the type of input expected, such as text, email, date, etc.

2. **Form Validation**: Django provides built-in methods to validate user input, ensuring that the data submitted is correct.

3. **Form Rendering**: Django allows rendering forms automatically into HTML, and provides tools to customize their appearance.

Forms are essential for capturing data from users, whether it's for creating or editing records, logging in, submitting comments, or any other type of user interaction that involves data input.

Creating Forms for User Input

There are two main ways to create forms in Django: **manual forms** (using `forms.Form`) and **model-based forms** (using `forms.ModelForm`).

1. Creating a Simple Form with `forms.Form`

To create a basic form in Django, you need to define a class that inherits from `forms.Form`. This class defines the fields you want to collect from the user. Each field is an instance of a `forms.Field` class, such as `CharField`, `EmailField`, `IntegerField`, and more.

Example of a Simple Form:

```python
python
```

91

```
from django import forms

class ContactForm(forms.Form):
    name = forms.CharField(max_length=100)
    email = forms.EmailField()
    message                                =
forms.CharField(widget=forms.Textarea)
```

- `CharField`: Used for a short text field, such as a name or subject.
- `EmailField`: Used for an email input, automatically checking if the input is a valid email format.
- `Textarea`: Used for a multi-line text input field, suitable for a longer message.

2. Creating a Form Based on a Model with `forms.ModelForm`

If you're working with a Django model (e.g., a `Post` model), you can automatically generate a form based on the model using `forms.ModelForm`. This is especially useful when you need to create or update database records.

Example of a ModelForm:

```python
from django import forms
```

92

```
from .models import Post

class PostForm(forms.ModelForm):
    class Meta:
        model = Post
        fields = ['title', 'content']
```

- **ModelForm**: By using `forms.ModelForm`, you can generate a form that corresponds directly to the fields of your model.
- **Meta Class**: Inside the `PostForm`, the `Meta` class specifies which model the form is based on (`Post`) and which fields should be included in the form.

Validating and Saving Form Data

Once a form is created, you need to handle user input, validate it, and save it to the database (if necessary).

1. Validating Form Data

Validation in Django is automatic for common field types. For example:

- **EmailField** will check if the email is in the correct format.
- **IntegerField** will ensure the value entered is an integer.

Django also provides custom validation methods that allow you to define rules specific to your application.

93

Example of Validating a Simple Form:

python

```
from django.shortcuts import render
from .forms import ContactForm

def contact_view(request):
    if request.method == 'POST':
        form = ContactForm(request.POST)
        if form.is_valid():    # Automatically
checks all fields
            name = form.cleaned_data['name']
            email = form.cleaned_data['email']
            message                          =
form.cleaned_data['message']
            # Handle the valid data, e.g., send
an email
            return               render(request,
'thank_you.html', {'name': name})
    else:
        form = ContactForm()
    return     render(request,     'contact.html',
{'form': form})
```

In this example:

- `form.is_valid()` performs validation on all fields in the form. If any field contains invalid data (e.g., an improperly formatted email), the form is considered invalid.

- `form.cleaned_data` is a dictionary containing the cleaned (validated) data from the form. This is where you retrieve the user-provided values for further processing.

2. Custom Validation for a Form Field

Django allows you to add custom validation to specific form fields. This is useful if you need to enforce custom rules that aren't provided by default.

Example of Custom Validation for a Form Field:

python

```python
class ContactForm(forms.Form):
    name = forms.CharField(max_length=100)
    email = forms.EmailField()
    message =
forms.CharField(widget=forms.Textarea)

    def clean_message(self):
        message =
self.cleaned_data.get('message')
        if len(message) < 10:
            raise forms.ValidationError('Message
must be at least 10 characters long.')
        return message
```

In this example, the `clean_message` method is a custom validation method for the `message` field. If the message is shorter than 10 characters, it raises a `ValidationError`.

3. Saving Form Data

Once the form is valid, you can save the data to your database (if the form is related to a model). For `ModelForm`, saving is simple:

Saving Data from a ModelForm:

python

```python
def post_create(request):
    if request.method == 'POST':
        form = PostForm(request.POST)
        if form.is_valid():
            form.save()  # Saves the new Post to
the database
            return redirect('post_list')
    else:
        form = PostForm()
    return render(request, 'post_form.html',
{'form': form})
```

In this example:

- `form.save()` automatically creates a new instance of the `Post` model and saves it to the database.

For non-model forms (i.e., using `forms.Form`), you can manually save the data to the database or process it however you need.

Example of Saving Non-Model Form Data:

python

```
def contact_view(request):
    if request.method == 'POST':
        form = ContactForm(request.POST)
        if form.is_valid():
            name = form.cleaned_data['name']
            email = form.cleaned_data['email']
            message                              =
form.cleaned_data['message']
            # Example of saving to a custom model
or sending an email

ContactMessage.objects.create(name=name,
email=email, message=message)
            return              render(request,
'thank_you.html', {'name': name})
    else:
        form = ContactForm()
    return    render(request,    'contact.html',
{'form': form})
```

In this example, the cleaned data is manually saved to a custom model `ContactMessage`.

Handling Forms in Templates

To display a form on a web page, you render it in a template. Django forms can be rendered using {{ form }} to output the entire form automatically, or you can manually render individual fields.

Example of Rendering a Form in a Template:

html

```
<form method="POST">
    {% csrf_token %}
    {{ form.as_p }} <!-- Renders the form as a
series of <p> elements -->
    <button type="submit">Submit</button>
</form>
```

- {% csrf_token %} is important for security. It prevents Cross-Site Request Forgery (CSRF) attacks by adding a hidden token to the form that is checked when the form is submitted.

- {{ form.as_p }} renders the form fields inside <p> tags. You can also use {{ form.as_table }} for rendering as a table or manually render each field like {{ form.name }}.

Summary

In this chapter, we covered the basics of working with forms in Django. We explored how to create forms for user input using both `forms.Form` and `forms.ModelForm`, how to validate form data, and how to save valid data to the database. Additionally, we discussed rendering forms in templates and handling user submissions securely.

Django's form system simplifies the process of capturing and processing user input, handling common tasks like validation and saving data to the database, so you can focus on building your application's functionality. As you continue to develop more complex forms, you'll be able to take advantage of Django's built-in tools for customizing validation and improving the user experience.

CHAPTER 10

DJANGO ADMIN INTERFACE

The **Django Admin Interface** is one of Django's most powerful and useful features. It allows you to manage and interact with the data in your application through a web-based interface. In this chapter, we will cover how to use Django's built-in admin interface, how to customize it to suit your needs, and how to manage content efficiently through the admin panel.

Using Django's Built-in Admin Interface

Django provides a fully functional, web-based admin interface that you can use to manage the data in your application. This interface is automatically generated from the models defined in your project, allowing you to perform CRUD operations (Create, Read, Update, Delete) on your data without writing any additional code.

1. Enabling the Admin Interface

To use the admin interface, you need to follow these steps:

- **Step 1: Add** `'django.contrib.admin'` **to** `INSTALLED_APPS`

Make sure that `django.contrib.admin` is included in the `INSTALLED_APPS` setting in your `settings.py` file:

```python
python
```

```python
INSTALLED_APPS = [
    # Other apps
    'django.contrib.admin',
    'django.contrib.auth',
    'django.contrib.contenttypes',
    'django.contrib.sessions',
    'django.contrib.messages',
    'django.contrib.staticfiles',
]
```

- **Step 2: Register Models in the Admin Panel**

To make a model available in the admin interface, you need to register it with the admin site. This is done in the `admin.py` file of your app.

For example, to register a `Post` model, you would write the following in `myapp/admin.py`:

```python
python
```

```python
from django.contrib import admin
from .models import Post
```

```
admin.site.register(Post)
```

By default, Django will generate a basic interface to create, read, update, and delete `Post` objects.

- **Step 3: Create a Superuser**

To access the admin interface, you need to create a superuser account. Run the following command to create a superuser:

```bash
bash
```

```
python manage.py createsuperuser
```

Follow the prompts to set up the username, email, and password for the superuser account.

- **Step 4: Start the Development Server**

Run the server with the following command:

```bash
bash
```

```
python manage.py runserver
```

Now, open your web browser and navigate to `http://127.0.0.1:8000/admin`. Log in using the superuser credentials, and you will be able to manage your data through the admin interface.

Customizing the Admin Panel

The Django admin interface provides a basic, but customizable, interface out of the box. You can enhance the admin panel's functionality and appearance by customizing the way models are displayed, adding search functionality, and more.

1. Customizing Model Display in Admin

By default, Django's admin interface provides a simple list of models and their fields. However, you can customize the admin interface to control which fields are displayed, how the data is presented, and how you can interact with it.

Here's an example of how to customize the `Post` model display:

python

```python
from django.contrib import admin
from .models import Post

class PostAdmin(admin.ModelAdmin):
    list_display    =    ('title',    'author',
'published_date')  # Display these fields in the
list view
    list_filter = ('author', 'published_date')  #
Add filter options in the sidebar
    search_fields  =  ('title',  'content')    #
Enable search by title and content
```

```
ordering = ('-published_date',)    # Default
ordering by published date in descending order
```

```
admin.site.register(Post, PostAdmin)
```

Explanation of Customizations:

- **list_display**: Specifies the fields to display in the list view of the admin panel.
- **list_filter**: Adds filter options in the sidebar to filter the list by certain fields.
- **search_fields**: Enables a search bar to search for specific terms within the specified fields.
- **ordering**: Sets the default ordering of records in the list view.

2. Adding Inline Forms to Admin

If your model has a relationship with another model (e.g., a ForeignKey or ManyToManyField), you can display related models directly in the admin interface using inline forms.

Example of Inline Form for Related Models:

```python
from django.contrib import admin
from .models import Post, Comment
```

```python
class CommentInline(admin.TabularInline):
    model = Comment
    extra = 1  # Adds one empty form for adding
new comments


class PostAdmin(admin.ModelAdmin):
    list_display    =    ('title',    'author',
'published_date')
    inlines = [CommentInline]  # Display related
comments directly in the Post admin page


admin.site.register(Post, PostAdmin)
```

In this example, CommentInline is used to display Comment instances within the Post admin page.

3. Customizing Forms in the Admin

You can also customize the forms that appear in the admin interface. For example, you can change the layout, fieldsets, or even add custom widgets to specific fields.

Example of Customizing Forms in the Admin:

```python
python

from django import forms
from django.contrib import admin
from .models import Post
```

```
class PostForm(forms.ModelForm):
    class Meta:
        model = Post
        fields = ['title', 'content', 'author']

    def clean_title(self):
        title = self.cleaned_data['title']
        if "Django" not in title:
            raise      forms.ValidationError('The
title must contain the word "Django".')
        return title

class PostAdmin(admin.ModelAdmin):
    form = PostForm
    list_display    =    ('title',    'author',
'published_date')

admin.site.register(Post, PostAdmin)
```

In this example:

- **Custom form**: PostForm is used to apply custom validation to the title field. The validation checks if the title contains the word "Django".
- **form**: This is specified in PostAdmin to use the custom form.

4. Customizing the Admin Interface's Appearance

You can modify the appearance of the admin interface using CSS or by overriding default templates. For more advanced customizations, you may create your own templates and override the default admin templates.

To add custom CSS to the admin panel, you can use the `Media` class:

```python
python

class PostAdmin(admin.ModelAdmin):
    class Media:
        css = {
            'all': ('myapp/css/admin.css',)
        }

admin.site.register(Post, PostAdmin)
```

This will apply the custom CSS defined in `myapp/css/admin.css` to the admin interface.

Managing Content Through the Admin Interface

Once you've registered your models and set up the admin interface, you can use it to manage your content easily. The admin panel provides a user-friendly interface for creating, editing, and deleting records in your database.

1. Creating Records

To create a new record, navigate to the appropriate model in the admin panel and click the "Add" button. This will bring up a form where you can input the data for the new record. Once you fill out the form, click the "Save" button to save the record to the database.

2. Editing Records

To edit a record, click on the record you want to modify in the list view. This will open up the form with the current data pre-filled. Make the necessary changes and click "Save" to update the record.

3. Deleting Records

To delete a record, select the checkbox next to the record(s) in the list view, and then click the "Delete" button. Django will ask for confirmation before deleting the selected record(s).

4. Bulk Actions

Django's admin interface also supports bulk actions. You can select multiple records and perform actions like deletion or marking them as active/inactive.

5. Using the Admin Interface for User Management

The admin interface can also be used to manage users and groups. Django provides built-in models for user authentication (User model) and permissions, allowing you to add, edit, and remove users and assign roles (permissions).

You can access user management through the "Users" section in the admin interface.

Summary

In this chapter, we explored the Django admin interface and how to use it to manage your application's data. We discussed how to register models for use in the admin, customize the admin interface to suit your needs, and use the admin panel to manage content effectively. Customizing the admin interface allows you to tailor it to your specific needs, while using it for content management ensures that your application's data is easy to handle.

The Django admin interface is an invaluable tool for developers and administrators, streamlining data management and providing a robust, easy-to-use interface to handle your application's content.

CHAPTER 11

WORKING WITH STATIC FILES AND MEDIA

In web development, **static files** (such as CSS, JavaScript, and images) are essential for the structure, design, and interactivity of your website. Django provides an efficient way to manage and serve static files and media content. In this chapter, we will cover how to manage static files (CSS, JS), handle media files (images, videos), and best practices for serving static content.

Managing Static Files (CSS, JS)

Static files are files that don't change during the course of the user's interaction with a website. These files are typically used for styling (CSS), scripting (JavaScript), and including assets like images. Django provides a simple way to manage and serve these files, but they must be set up correctly in both development and production environments.

1. Setting Up Static Files in Django

To manage static files, you need to configure Django's static file settings in `settings.py`.

- **Static Files Directory**: In development, static files are often placed in a `static` directory within each app or at the project level. Django needs to know where these files are located.

In `settings.py`, add the following settings:

```python
python

STATIC_URL = '/static/'

# Directory where static files will be stored in development
STATICFILES_DIRS = [
    BASE_DIR / "static",  # This will look for the static directory in the root of the project
]

# Directory where static files will be collected in production (e.g., for serving them via a CDN)
STATIC_ROOT = BASE_DIR / "staticfiles"
```

- **STATIC_URL**: This defines the URL that will be used to access static files in your templates, such as `/static/css/style.css`.
- **STATICFILES_DIRS**: A list of directories where Django will search for additional static files during development.

- **STATIC_ROOT**: The directory where static files will be collected when preparing for production. This is used when running `python manage.py collectstatic` to gather all static files into a single directory for serving in production.

2. Including Static Files in Templates

To include static files (CSS, JS, etc.) in your templates, use the `{% load static %}` tag. This tells Django to insert the correct path to the static file.

Example of Including a CSS File in a Template:

html

```
{% load static %}
<!DOCTYPE html>
<html>
<head>
    <title>My Site</title>
    <link    rel="stylesheet"    type="text/css"
href="{% static 'css/styles.css' %}">
</head>
<body>
    <h1>Welcome to My Site</h1>
</body>
</html>
```

In this example:

- `{% load static %}` loads Django's static files handling system.
- `{% static 'css/styles.css' %}` generates the URL for the static file located in the `static/css/` directory.

3. Serving Static Files in Development

During development, Django can serve static files directly by running the development server. However, in production, it's common to serve static files using a more efficient web server (e.g., Nginx or Apache).

To serve static files in development, ensure that `django.contrib.staticfiles` is included in your `INSTALLED_APPS`, and use the `runserver` command:

```bash

python manage.py runserver
```

Django will automatically serve static files from the directories specified in `STATICFILES_DIRS` and provide them via the `/static/` URL.

4. Collecting Static Files for Production

In production, static files should be served by a dedicated web server (e.g., Nginx or Apache) for better performance. To prepare static files for production, you need to run the `collectstatic` command:

```bash

python manage.py collectstatic
```

This command collects all static files from the directories specified in `STATICFILES_DIRS` and places them in the `STATIC_ROOT` directory. After running this command, you can configure your production server to serve these static files efficiently.

Handling Media Files (Images, Videos)

Media files are user-uploaded files such as images, videos, PDFs, and other documents. These files are different from static files because they are dynamic and can change with each user interaction.

1. Configuring Media File Settings

In Django, you need to specify where to store media files and how to access them. Add the following settings to `settings.py` to configure media file handling:

114

```
python

MEDIA_URL = '/media/'
MEDIA_ROOT = BASE_DIR / 'media'
```

- **MEDIA_URL**: This defines the URL that will be used to access media files, such as /media/uploads/image.jpg.
- **MEDIA_ROOT**: This is the file system path where media files will be stored. It can be any directory where you want to store uploaded files.

2. Handling Media File Uploads in Forms

Django provides a simple way to handle file uploads in forms. You can define a `FileField` or `ImageField` in your model to allow users to upload files.

Example of a Model with an ImageField:

```
python

from django.db import models

class Post(models.Model):
    title = models.CharField(max_length=100)
    content = models.TextField()
    image                                    =
models.ImageField(upload_to='posts/images/')
```

115

In this example:

- The `ImageField` is used to upload images.
- The `upload_to='posts/images/'` parameter specifies that the uploaded files will be stored in the `media/posts/images/` directory.

3. Handling File Uploads in Forms

To allow users to upload files, you need to include an `enctype="multipart/form-data"` attribute in the HTML form tag.

Example of an HTML Form with File Upload:

```html
<form method="POST" enctype="multipart/form-data">
    {% csrf_token %}
    {{ form.as_p }}
    <button type="submit">Submit</button>
</form>
```

4. Displaying Media Files in Templates

Once a file is uploaded and stored, you can display it in your templates by referencing the media URL.

Example of Displaying an Image in a Template:

html

```
<img src="{{ post.image.url }}" alt="Post Image">
```

In this example, `{{ post.image.url }}` generates the URL to access the uploaded image. The URL is constructed using the `MEDIA_URL` setting.

5. Serving Media Files in Development

During development, Django can serve media files through the `media` directory. Add the following configuration to your `urls.py` to serve media files:

python

```
from django.conf import settings
from django.conf.urls.static import static
from django.urls import path

urlpatterns = [
    # Other URL patterns
]

# Serve media files in development
if settings.DEBUG:
```

117

```
urlpatterns += static(settings.MEDIA_URL,
document_root=settings.MEDIA_ROOT)
```

This allows Django to serve media files at the `/media/` URL during development.

6. Serving Media Files in Production

In production, media files should be served by a dedicated web server like Nginx or Apache, which is more efficient than Django's built-in development server.

You will need to configure your production web server to serve files from the `MEDIA_ROOT` directory, using the URL defined in `MEDIA_URL`.

Best Practices for Serving Static Content

While Django's development server provides basic static and media file handling, serving static content efficiently in a production environment requires best practices to ensure scalability and performance.

1. Use a Dedicated Web Server for Static Files

In production, static files should be served by a high-performance web server like Nginx or Apache, rather than Django itself. These web servers are optimized for serving static content and can handle large volumes of traffic more effectively than Django.

2. Use a Content Delivery Network (CDN)

A **Content Delivery Network (CDN)** is a network of servers distributed across various geographical locations. Using a CDN can improve the speed and reliability of serving static files (such as images, CSS, and JavaScript), especially for global users. A CDN caches static files on servers closer to the user, reducing latency.

You can configure Django to use a CDN for static files by updating the `STATIC_URL` setting to point to the CDN URL:

python

```
STATIC_URL = 'https://mycdn.com/static/'
```

3. Enable Caching for Static Files

To optimize static file delivery, enable caching so that files are stored in the user's browser for a longer period. You can add caching headers to your static files via your web server (Nginx or Apache). For example, set the `Cache-Control` header to instruct the browser to cache static files for a specified duration.

4. Compress Static Files

Compressing static files (such as CSS, JavaScript, and images) reduces their size and speeds up loading times. You can use tools like **Gzip** or **Brotli** to compress your static files before serving them. Many web servers, such as Nginx, have built-in support for serving compressed files.

5. Secure File Uploads

When handling media file uploads, it is essential to ensure that users can't upload malicious files. Always validate the file type, file size, and extension before saving media files to your server.

6. Store Media Files Separately from Static Files

Media files (uploads) should be stored in a different directory from static files. This makes it easier to manage user-generated content and provides greater flexibility when configuring access and permissions.

Summary

In this chapter, we covered how to manage static and media files in Django. We learned how to configure static files for CSS and JavaScript, as well as how to handle user-uploaded media files such as images and videos. We also discussed best practices for serving static content efficiently, including using a dedicated web server, CDNs, caching, and file compression.

By following these practices and properly configuring your static and media files, you can optimize the performance, security, and scalability of your Django application, providing a seamless user experience.

CHAPTER 12

UNDERSTANDING DJANGO'S AUTHENTICATION SYSTEM

Django provides a powerful and flexible authentication system that allows you to manage user authentication, handle user sessions, and secure your web application. In this chapter, we'll explore how Django's built-in authentication system works, how to create user registration and login forms, and how to manage user sessions and ensure the security of your application.

User Authentication in Django

Authentication refers to the process of verifying a user's identity. In Django, the authentication system handles tasks like user login, user registration, and managing sessions.

Django includes the `django.contrib.auth` module, which provides a ready-to-use solution for handling user authentication. It includes models, views, and forms for user login, registration, and management. The core components of Django's authentication system are:

1. **User Model**: The default model provided by Django that stores user information (e.g., username, password, email).

2. **Authentication Views**: Views for logging users in and out, such as `LoginView` and `LogoutView`.

3. **Forms**: Forms for user login and registration.

4. **Sessions**: Django uses sessions to keep track of logged-in users, so they don't need to log in on every page request.

Django provides a high-level abstraction to manage user authentication out of the box, allowing you to focus on the specifics of your application without having to handle low-level authentication tasks manually.

Creating User Registration and Login Forms

In most web applications, users need to create accounts, log in, and log out. Django provides tools for these tasks, but you may need to customize forms for your application.

1. Creating a User Registration Form

To allow users to register on your site, you need to create a form that takes in the user's information and saves it to the database.

Django provides a built-in `UserCreationForm` for user registration, which includes fields for the username, password, and password confirmation. You can extend this form to include additional fields such as email.

Example of a User Registration Form:

```python
python

from        django.contrib.auth.forms        import
UserCreationForm
from django import forms
from django.contrib.auth.models import User

class
CustomUserRegistrationForm(UserCreationForm):
    email = forms.EmailField(required=True)

    class Meta:
        model = User
        fields    =    ['username',    'email',
'password1', 'password2']
```

- **UserCreationForm**: This form is pre-built to handle user registration and includes validation for the password fields (e.g., checking that both passwords match).
- **Custom Fields**: We added an `email` field to the form to allow users to provide their email during registration.

2. Handling User Registration in the View

Once you have the registration form, you need to handle the form submission and create the user in the database. Here's how you can create a view for user registration:

```python
python
```

```python
from django.shortcuts import render, redirect
from .forms import CustomUserRegistrationForm

def register(request):
    if request.method == 'POST':
        form = CustomUserRegistrationForm(request.POST)
        if form.is_valid():
            form.save()  # Save the new user
            return redirect('login')  # Redirect to login page after successful registration
    else:
        form = CustomUserRegistrationForm()

    return render(request, 'registration/register.html', {'form': form})
```

In this view:

- **POST Request**: When the form is submitted, the user's data is validated and saved to the database if the form is valid.
- **redirect('login')**: After the user is successfully registered, they are redirected to the login page.

3. Creating a User Login Form

125

Django provides a built-in `AuthenticationForm` that handles user login. This form contains fields for the username and password and automatically validates the credentials.

Example of a User Login Form:

python

```python
from       django.contrib.auth.forms        import
AuthenticationForm
from django.shortcuts import render, redirect
from django.contrib.auth import login

def login_view(request):
    if request.method == 'POST':
        form   =   AuthenticationForm(request,
data=request.POST)
        if form.is_valid():
            user = form.get_user()  # Get the
authenticated user
            login(request, user)  # Log the user
in
            return redirect('home')  # Redirect
to a homepage or dashboard after successful login
    else:
        form = AuthenticationForm()

    return                       render(request,
'registration/login.html', {'form': form})
```

126

In this view:

- **AuthenticationForm**: This form validates the username and password against the user records in the database.
- **login()**: Once the user is authenticated, the `login()` function logs them in by creating a session.

Managing User Sessions and Security

Once users are authenticated, Django manages their sessions automatically, so they don't need to log in repeatedly. However, managing user sessions securely is important to prevent unauthorized access and protect user data.

1. Django Sessions

Django uses sessions to track whether a user is logged in or not. A session is created when a user successfully logs in, and the session persists across page requests. By default, Django stores session data in a database table called `django_session`.

Session Settings in `settings.py`:

```python
SESSION_ENGINE                                    =
'django.contrib.sessions.backends.db'   # Store
sessions in the database
```

127

```
SESSION_COOKIE_AGE = 3600  # Session timeout (in seconds)
```

- **SESSION_ENGINE**: This setting defines how session data is stored. By default, Django uses a database-backed session store.
- **SESSION_COOKIE_AGE**: This controls the duration (in seconds) that the session remains active. After the session expires, the user will be logged out automatically.

2. Protecting Against Session Fixation

Session fixation occurs when an attacker sets a user's session ID to a known value, allowing them to hijack the session. Django provides protection against session fixation by default. When a user logs in, Django automatically generates a new session ID to prevent session fixation attacks.

3. Logging Out a User

Django provides a simple way to log out a user. When a user logs out, the session is cleared, and they are redirected to another page.

Example of Logging Out a User:

```python
from django.contrib.auth import logout
from django.shortcuts import redirect
```

```
def logout_view(request):
    logout(request)  # Logs the user out
    return redirect('login')  # Redirect to the
login page
```

- **logout()**: This function logs out the user and clears their session.

4. Password Management

Django's authentication system includes secure password storage and management features. Passwords are stored in the database as hashed values using a strong hashing algorithm (PBKDF2 by default).

- **Password Change**: Django includes built-in views and forms for changing the password. You can use PasswordChangeForm for handling password changes.

Example of a Password Change View:

```
python
```

```
from      django.contrib.auth.forms      import
PasswordChangeForm
from          django.contrib.auth          import
update_session_auth_hash
```

```
def password_change_view(request):
    if request.method == 'POST':
        form = PasswordChangeForm(request.user,
request.POST)
        if form.is_valid():
            form.save()  # Save the new password
            update_session_auth_hash(request,
form.user)  # Keep the user logged in after
changing the password
            return
redirect('password_change_done')
    else:
        form = PasswordChangeForm(request.user)

    return                         render(request,
'registration/password_change.html',    {'form':
form})
```

- **update_session_auth_hash()**: This function ensures the user remains logged in after changing their password by updating the session's authentication hash.

Security Considerations

When working with Django's authentication system, consider the following security practices:

1. **Use HTTPS**: Always use HTTPS (SSL/TLS) to secure communication between the client and server, especially

130

for login and password forms. This prevents attackers from intercepting sensitive data.

2. **Limit Login Attempts**: Consider implementing a mechanism to limit failed login attempts to prevent brute force attacks. There are third-party Django apps available, such as `django-axes`, that can help with this.

3. **Enable Two-Factor Authentication (2FA)**: For extra security, you can integrate two-factor authentication in your application. Django provides support for this via third-party packages like `django-otp`.

4. **Use Django's Built-In Security Features**: Django includes many built-in security features, such as protection against CSRF (Cross-Site Request Forgery), clickjacking, and session fixation. Ensure these features are enabled by keeping your Django settings secure.

Summary

In this chapter, we explored Django's built-in authentication system, including how to create user registration and login forms, manage user sessions, and ensure the security of your application. We also discussed best practices for handling passwords, protecting against session fixation, and maintaining secure user authentication workflows.

Django's authentication system simplifies the management of user identities and security, providing a robust framework for implementing secure, user-friendly login and registration features in your web applications.

CHAPTER 13

DJANGO VIEWS –
UNDERSTANDING REQUEST AND
RESPONSE

Django views are central to the web framework's functionality. A view is a Python function that processes a web request and returns a web response. This chapter will explore how Django processes requests and responses, the role of request and response objects, and how to modify and return responses in Django.

How Django Processes Requests and Responses

When a user sends a request to a Django-powered website, Django processes the request by matching the requested URL with the appropriate view function. The view then processes the request and returns a response.

The request-response cycle in Django works as follows:

1. **Request is Received**: When a user visits a URL, the browser sends an HTTP request to the Django server.

2. **URL Matching**: Django uses URL patterns defined in the `urls.py` file to map the requested URL to a specific view function.

3. **View Processing**: The view function processes the request, which may involve querying a database, handling form data, or performing any other necessary operations.

4. **Response is Returned**: The view function returns an HTTP response, typically rendered as an HTML page, but it could also return JSON, a file, or any other type of data.

5. **Response is Sent**: Django sends the response back to the user's browser, which renders it as a webpage.

Example Request-Response Cycle:

- **Request**: The user visits `http://example.com/blog/`.

- **URL Matching**: Django maps `/blog/` to the `blog_view` function.

- **View Processing**: The `blog_view` function queries the database for blog posts.

- **Response**: Django renders a template with the blog posts and returns an HTTP response.

- **Sending Response**: The response is sent to the user's browser, where the blog posts are displayed.

The Role of Request Objects and Response Objects

In Django, both **request objects** and **response objects** play vital roles in processing and handling HTTP requests and responses.

1. Request Objects

The **request object** represents the incoming HTTP request from the user. It contains all the data sent by the client (the user's browser) to the server. The request object is passed automatically to every view function in Django.

Key attributes of the request object include:

- `request.method`: The HTTP method used for the request (e.g., `GET`, `POST`, `PUT`, `DELETE`).
- `request.GET`: A dictionary-like object that contains data sent in the URL's query string for `GET` requests.
- `request.POST`: A dictionary-like object that contains data sent in the body of the request for `POST` requests (typically form data).
- `request.COOKIES`: A dictionary-like object containing cookies sent by the browser.
- `request.FILES`: A dictionary-like object containing files uploaded in the request (such as images or documents).

- **request.user**: The user who is making the request (if the user is authenticated). This allows you to access the currently logged-in user.

Example: Accessing Data from a Request:

python

```
def example_view(request):
    # Accessing query parameters from the URL
(e.g., ?name=John)
    name = request.GET.get('name', 'Guest')    #
Default to 'Guest' if 'name' is not provided
    return HttpResponse(f'Hello, {name}!')
```

In this example:

- The request.GET.get('name') retrieves the value of the name query parameter from the URL.

2. Response Objects

The **response object** represents the outgoing HTTP response that is returned to the client's browser. It contains the content to be sent back, along with additional headers such as content type, status code, and more.

The most common types of response objects in Django are:

- **HttpResponse**: The basic response class, used to return simple content like HTML, plain text, or JSON.
- **JsonResponse**: A subclass of HttpResponse that returns data in JSON format (useful for APIs).
- **HttpResponseRedirect**: A response class that sends an HTTP redirect to a different URL.
- **render**: A shortcut function that combines rendering a template and returning an HTTP response.

Example of a Basic Response:

python

```python
from django.http import HttpResponse

def hello_view(request):
    return HttpResponse('Hello, world!')
```

In this example:

- The HttpResponse object returns the text "Hello, world!" as the response to the user.

Modifying and Returning Responses

Django provides multiple ways to modify and customize the response sent to the client. You can change the content, set headers, or perform redirects, among other actions.

1. Returning Dynamic Content with Templates

Django allows you to render dynamic HTML content using templates. The `render` function is the most common way to generate a response from a template.

Example: Rendering a Template as a Response:

```python
python

from django.shortcuts import render

def blog_view(request):
    posts = Post.objects.all()  # Retrieve blog posts from the database
    return render(request, 'blog.html', {'posts': posts})
```

In this example:

- The `render` function combines the `blog.html` template with the context data (in this case, a list of `posts`), generating an HTML page to return as the response.

2. Redirecting to Another URL

Sometimes, after processing a request (such as submitting a form), you may want to redirect the user to another URL. Django provides a `HttpResponseRedirect` class for this.

Example: Redirecting a User:

```python
python

from django.shortcuts import redirect

def post_create(request):
    if request.method == 'POST':
        # Save new post
        form.save()
        return redirect('post_list')  # Redirect
to the post list view
    return render(request, 'post_create.html',
{'form': form})
```

In this example:

- After a successful form submission, the user is redirected to the list of posts.

3. Setting Response Headers

You can modify the response headers to provide additional information to the client. For example, you can set the `Content-Type` header to specify the type of content being returned, or you can enable caching.

Example: Setting Custom Headers:

```python
python

from django.http import HttpResponse

def custom_headers_view(request):
    response = HttpResponse('This is a response
with custom headers.')
    response['X-Custom-Header']        =
'MyCustomHeaderValue'  # Set a custom header
    return response
```

In this example:

- A custom header (X-Custom-Header) is added to the response.

4. Returning JSON Responses

Django provides the JsonResponse class for returning data in JSON format. This is commonly used for APIs or when responding with structured data.

Example: Returning a JSON Response:

```python
python

from django.http import JsonResponse

def api_view(request):
    data = {
```

```
        'message': 'Hello, world!',
        'status': 'success'
    }
    return JsonResponse(data)
```

In this example:

- A `JsonResponse` is returned with a dictionary converted into JSON format.

5. Returning a File Response

Django also provides the `FileResponse` class to return files (such as PDFs or images) as part of the response.

Example: Returning a File Response:

python

```
from django.http import FileResponse

def download_view(request):
    file_path = 'path/to/file.pdf'
    return FileResponse(open(file_path, 'rb'),
content_type='application/pdf')
```

In this example:

- A PDF file is opened and returned as a `FileResponse`, allowing the user to download it.

141

Summary

In this chapter, we explored the core concepts of **requests and responses** in Django. We learned how Django processes incoming requests, how request objects carry data from the client, and how response objects hold the data that will be sent back to the client. We also covered how to modify responses, including returning dynamic content via templates, performing redirects, setting custom headers, returning JSON data, and serving files.

Django's request and response handling system is highly flexible and can be customized to meet the needs of your application. Understanding how to use and manipulate these objects is crucial for building dynamic, interactive, and secure web applications.

CHAPTER 14

DJANGO TEMPLATES –
ADVANCED TEMPLATE
FEATURES

Django's template system provides a powerful way to render dynamic content, separate the application's logic from presentation, and create reusable components. In this chapter, we'll explore some advanced template features, including **template inheritance**, **creating reusable templates**, and **using custom template filters and tags**. These features allow you to write cleaner, more maintainable, and flexible templates for your Django application.

Template Inheritance

Template inheritance allows you to create a base template that defines common structure (e.g., header, footer, navigation) and then extend it in other templates. This helps you avoid repetitive code by reusing common elements across multiple pages.

1. Basic Template Inheritance

Django's template inheritance system works by defining a base template with placeholder blocks that can be overridden in child templates.

- **Base Template (`base.html`)**:

html

```html
<!DOCTYPE html>
<html>
<head>
    <title>{% block title %}My Site{% endblock %}</title>
</head>
<body>
    <header>
        <h1>Welcome to My Site</h1>
        <nav>
            <ul>
                <li><a href="/">Home</a></li>
                <li><a href="/about/">About</a></li>
                <li><a href="/contact/">Contact</a></li>
            </ul>
        </nav>
    </header>

    <div>
```

```
    {% block content %}{% endblock %}
</div>

<footer>
    <p>My Site &; 2025</p>
</footer>
</body>
</html>
```

- **Child Template (`home.html`):**

html

```
{% extends 'base.html' %}

{% block title %}Home{% endblock %}

{% block content %}
    <h2>Welcome to the homepage!</h2>
    <p>This is the content of the homepage.</p>
{% endblock %}
```

In this example:

- **`{% extends 'base.html' %}`**: The child template inherits from `base.html`.
- **`{% block title %}` and `{% block content %}`:** These blocks allow child templates to override the title and content sections of the base template.

2. Using Multiple Blocks

You can define as many blocks as needed in the base template, allowing child templates to override different parts of the layout.

- **Example with multiple blocks:**

html

```
{% block header %}Header content here{% endblock %}
{% block footer %}Footer content here{% endblock %}
```

Creating Reusable Templates

Reusable templates allow you to encapsulate common structures and components (such as forms, sidebars, or navigation) in separate templates that can be included in multiple pages. This promotes cleaner code and avoids duplication.

1. Using `{% include %}` to Reuse Template Components

The `{% include %}` tag allows you to include one template inside another. It is useful for reusing components like headers, footers, or sidebars.

- **Example of Including a Sidebar Template (`sidebar.html`):**

html

```
<aside>
    <h3>Sidebar</h3>
    <ul>
        <li><a href="/profile/">Profile</a></li>
        <li><a
href="/settings/">Settings</a></li>
    </ul>
</aside>
```

- **In the Main Template (`home.html`):**

html

```
{% extends 'base.html' %}

{% block content %}
    <h2>Welcome to the homepage!</h2>
    <p>This is the content of the homepage.</p>

    {% include 'sidebar.html' %}   <!-- Include
the sidebar template here -->
{% endblock %}
```

In this example:

- The `sidebar.html` template is included inside the `home.html` template. This allows you to reuse the

147

sidebar across multiple pages without repeating the same code.

2. Passing Context to Included Templates

You can pass additional context variables to included templates, which is useful when you need to customize the included content.

- **Example of Passing Context to an Included Template**:

html

```
<!-- main.html -->
{% include 'sidebar.html' with
items=sidebar_items %}
```

- **In sidebar.html**:

html

```
<aside>
    <h3>Sidebar</h3>
    <ul>
        {% for item in items %}
            <li><a href="{{ item.url }}">{{
item.name }}</a></li>
        {% endfor %}
    </ul>
</aside>
```

148

In this case, `sidebar_items` is passed to `sidebar.html`, and the items are rendered dynamically.

Using Custom Template Filters and Tags

Django provides a set of built-in filters and tags to help you manipulate and display data. However, sometimes you may need custom functionality that is specific to your application. Django allows you to create custom template filters and tags to extend its templating system.

1. Creating Custom Template Filters

A **custom filter** allows you to modify or format data inside your templates. To create a custom filter, you need to write a Python function and register it with Django's template system.

- **Example of a Custom Filter**: Creating a filter that capitalizes the first letter of each word.
- **Filter Code (in templatetags/custom_filters.py)**:

```python
python

from django import template

register = template.Library()

@register.filter(name='capitalize_words')
```

149

```
def capitalize_words(value):
    return ' '.join([word.capitalize() for word
in value.split()])
```

- **Using the Filter in a Template**:

```
html

{% load custom_filters %}

<p>{{ 'hello world'|capitalize_words }}</p> <!-
- Output: 'Hello World' -->
```

- **Explanation**:
  - o `@register.filter(name='capitalize_w ords')`: This decorator registers the `capitalize_words` function as a custom template filter.
  - o In the template, we use `{% load custom_filters %}` to load the filter and apply it with `{{ 'hello world'|capitalize_words }}`.

2. Creating Custom Template Tags

A **custom template tag** is a way to add more complex functionality to your templates. Template tags can take arguments and perform logic before rendering content.

- **Example of a Custom Template Tag**: Creating a tag that returns the current year.
- **Tag Code (in `templatetags/custom_tags.py`)**:

python

```python
from django import template
import datetime

register = template.Library()

@register.simple_tag
def current_year():
    return datetime.datetime.now().year
```

- **Using the Template Tag in a Template**:

html

```html
{% load custom_tags %}

<p>The current year is: {% current_year %}</p>
```

- **Explanation**:
  - `@register.simple_tag`: This decorator registers the `current_year` function as a simple tag that can be used in templates.
  - `{% current_year %}` in the template calls the tag and displays the current year.

151

3. Customizing Template Tags with Arguments

You can create more advanced template tags that take arguments and perform more complex actions.

- **Example of a Custom Template Tag with Arguments**:

python

```
@register.simple_tag
def greeting(name):
    return f"Hello, {name}!"
```

- **Using the Tag with Arguments**:

html

```
{% load custom_tags %}

<p>{% greeting "John" %}</p>  <!-- Output: Hello, John! -->
```

In this example:

- The greeting tag takes a name argument and returns a personalized greeting.

Summary

In this chapter, we explored advanced Django template features that allow you to create flexible and reusable templates. We covered **template inheritance**, which allows you to define a base layout and extend it in child templates; **reusable templates** that can be included in multiple pages; and **custom template filters and tags**, which let you extend Django's template language with your own logic and functionality.

These advanced template features are essential for building scalable, maintainable Django applications. By leveraging inheritance, reusable components, and custom filters and tags, you can write cleaner, more modular code and improve the flexibility of your templates.

CHAPTER 15

BUILDING A RESTFUL API WITH DJANGO REST FRAMEWORK

Application Programming Interfaces (APIs) allow different systems or applications to communicate with each other. **REST** (Representational State Transfer) is an architectural style commonly used for designing networked applications, and Django Rest Framework (DRF) is a powerful toolkit for building Web APIs in Django. In this chapter, we'll walk through the basics of APIs and REST, how to set up Django Rest Framework, and how to build a simple API with DRF.

Introduction to APIs and REST

1. What is an API?

An **API** is a set of protocols, routines, and tools that allow software applications to communicate with each other. APIs define the methods and data formats for interactions between different software components. APIs are used to connect frontend and backend systems, third-party services, or different applications.

2. What is REST?

REST (Representational State Transfer) is an architectural style for building APIs. It relies on stateless communication between the client and server and is based on standard HTTP methods like **GET**, **POST**, **PUT**, **DELETE**, etc.

REST APIs are designed to handle the following:

- **Resources**: The objects (data) being manipulated by the API (e.g., users, posts, products).
- **HTTP Methods**: REST uses HTTP methods to interact with resources:
  - **GET**: Retrieve data from the server (e.g., get a list of blog posts).
  - **POST**: Create new data on the server (e.g., create a new blog post).
  - **PUT**: Update existing data (e.g., update a blog post).
  - **DELETE**: Remove data from the server (e.g., delete a blog post).
- **Stateless**: Each request from the client to the server must contain all the information needed to understand the request (e.g., authentication, data). The server does not store any session information between requests.

3. Why Use DRF for Building APIs?

Django Rest Framework (DRF) is a powerful toolkit that makes building RESTful APIs in Django faster and easier. DRF provides:

- Serialization: Converts Django models or Python data types into JSON format, which can be sent in HTTP responses.
- Authentication and Permissions: Built-in support for user authentication and controlling access to APIs.
- ViewSets and Routers: Simplified handling of common CRUD operations.
- Built-in support for common API patterns like pagination, filtering, and searching.

Setting Up Django Rest Framework (DRF)

To use Django Rest Framework, you first need to install it and add it to your Django project.

1. Installing DRF

Install Django Rest Framework using pip:

```bash

pip install djangorestframework
```

2. Adding DRF to Installed Apps

In your `settings.py` file, add `'rest_framework'` to the INSTALLED_APPS list:

python

```
INSTALLED_APPS = [
    # Other apps
    'rest_framework',
]
```

3. Setting Up the DRF Configuration

You can configure global settings for DRF, such as pagination, authentication, and permissions, by adding them to your `settings.py` file.

For example, to use the default authentication system and set pagination, you can add the following:

python

```
REST_FRAMEWORK = {
    'DEFAULT_AUTHENTICATION_CLASSES': [

'rest_framework.authentication.SessionAuthentic
ation',

'rest_framework.authentication.BasicAuthenticat
ion',
```

```
    ],
    'DEFAULT_PERMISSION_CLASSES': [

'rest_framework.permissions.IsAuthenticated',
    ],
    'PAGE_SIZE': 10   # Number of items per page
for pagination
}
```

4. Running Migrations

DRF uses Django's migration system to manage its internal database tables (like for token authentication). Run the following command to apply migrations:

```bash
bash
```

```
python manage.py migrate
```

Building a Simple API with DRF

Now that Django Rest Framework is set up, let's walk through building a simple API that provides access to a model's data.

1. Defining the Model

Let's define a simple model for blog posts that we'll expose through the API.

```python
python
```

```
from django.db import models

class Post(models.Model):
    title = models.CharField(max_length=100)
    content = models.TextField()
    published_date                          =
models.DateTimeField(auto_now_add=True)

    def __str__(self):
        return self.title
```

2. Creating a Serializer

Serializers are responsible for converting complex data types (like Django models) into JSON format and vice versa. DRF provides a powerful `ModelSerializer` that automatically generates serialization logic for model instances.

Here's how to create a serializer for the `Post` model:

```
python

from rest_framework import serializers
from .models import Post

class
PostSerializer(serializers.ModelSerializer):
    class Meta:
```

```
        model = Post
        fields = ['id', 'title', 'content',
'published_date']
```

In this example:

- **PostSerializer** inherits from serializers.ModelSerializer, which automatically generates the serializer fields based on the Post model.

3. Creating the View

Views in DRF handle HTTP requests and return API responses. The simplest way to create views for a model is by using **ViewSets**, which automatically provide the standard CRUD operations.

Here's how to create a view for the Post model:

python

```
from rest_framework import viewsets
from .models import Post
from .serializers import PostSerializer

class PostViewSet(viewsets.ModelViewSet):
    queryset = Post.objects.all()
    serializer_class = PostSerializer
```

In this example:

- **PostViewSet** inherits from `viewsets.ModelViewSet`, which automatically provides actions like `list`, `create`, `retrieve`, `update`, and `destroy`.
- **queryset**: This defines the list of objects that the view will operate on.
- **serializer_class**: This specifies the serializer to use for converting model instances to JSON.

4. Creating the URL Conf

To make the API available at a specific URL, you need to define the URL patterns. DRF provides a convenient `router` that automatically generates the URL patterns for `ViewSet` classes.

In your `urls.py`, add the following code:

python

```
from django.urls import path, include
from rest_framework.routers import DefaultRouter
from .views import PostViewSet

router = DefaultRouter()
router.register(r'posts', PostViewSet)
```

```
urlpatterns = [
    path('api/', include(router.urls)),
]
```

In this example:

- **DefaultRouter()**: Automatically generates URL patterns for the `PostViewSet`.
- **router.register()**: Registers the `PostViewSet` under the URL path `posts/`.

Now, the API will be accessible at `/api/posts/`, and the following endpoints will be available:

- **GET /api/posts/**: List all blog posts.
- **POST /api/posts/**: Create a new blog post.
- **GET /api/posts/{id}/**: Retrieve a specific blog post.
- **PUT /api/posts/{id}/**: Update a blog post.
- **DELETE /api/posts/{id}/**: Delete a blog post.

5. Testing the API

You can test the API using tools like **Postman** or **cURL** to make requests to the endpoints. For example:

- To list all posts:

  bash

162

```
GET http://127.0.0.1:8000/api/posts/
```

- To create a new post:

```bash
bash
```

```
POST http://127.0.0.1:8000/api/posts/
Content-Type: application/json
{
    "title": "New Post",
    "content": "This is the content of the
new post."
}
```

Summary

In this chapter, we covered how to build a simple **RESTful API** with Django Rest Framework (DRF). We learned how to:

- Set up Django Rest Framework in a Django project.
- Create a model and use DRF's `ModelSerializer` to serialize data.
- Use `ModelViewSet` to handle CRUD operations for a model.
- Define URLs using DRF's router to automatically generate the necessary API endpoints.

Django Rest Framework makes it easy to build and extend APIs with minimal code, and it provides a wide range of tools for handling authentication, permissions, pagination, and more. Now that you understand the basics of DRF, you can start building more complex and feature-rich APIs for your applications.

CHAPTER 16

HANDLING DATABASE MIGRATIONS

Database migrations are a crucial part of Django's ORM (Object-Relational Mapping) system, enabling you to manage changes to your database schema in a structured and organized way. Migrations allow you to evolve your database schema over time as your application changes without losing data. This chapter covers what migrations are, how to create and apply them, and best practices for managing migrations in Django.

What Are Migrations in Django?

Migrations are a way of propagating changes made to your Django models (such as adding new fields, deleting fields, or modifying the data types of existing fields) into the database. They provide a way to version-control database schema changes and ensure that all environments (development, staging, production) are synchronized with the latest database structure.

Django automatically generates migration files based on the changes you make to your models, and these migration files contain instructions for how to modify the database schema. Once a migration is created, you can apply it to your database to update its structure accordingly.

Key Concepts of Django Migrations:

- **Migration files**: Python files that contain database schema changes. They are stored in the `migrations` directory of each app.
- **Migration commands**: Commands like `makemigrations` and `migrate` that generate and apply migrations respectively.
- **Database schema changes**: Changes to models, like adding/removing fields or tables, changing field types, etc., which get translated into SQL statements through migrations.

Creating and Applying Migrations

1. Creating Migrations

Whenever you make changes to your Django models (such as adding, deleting, or modifying fields), Django needs to create migrations to reflect these changes in the database.

- **Step 1: Modify Your Models**

For example, let's say you have a `Post` model, and you add a new `author` field to it:

```python

from django.db import models

class Post(models.Model):
    title = models.CharField(max_length=100)
    content = models.TextField()
    author = models.CharField(max_length=100)   #
New field added
    published_date                              =
models.DateTimeField(auto_now_add=True)

    def __str__(self):
        return self.title
```

- **Step 2: Generate Migrations**

Once you have made changes to your models, you need to generate a migration file that will contain the database changes. You can generate migrations using the following command:

```bash

python manage.py makemigrations
```

This will create migration files in the `migrations` folder of the app containing the model changes. Django will detect changes to your models and generate the appropriate SQL operations to update the database schema.

167

- **Step 3: View the Generated Migration**

You can check the migration file that Django generated in your app's `migrations` folder. For example, it might look something like this:

```python
python

# migrations/0002_auto_20250712_1234.py

from django.db import migrations, models

class Migration(migrations.Migration):

    dependencies = [
        ('your_app_name', '0001_initial'),     # Referencing the previous migration
    ]

    operations = [
        migrations.AddField(
            model_name='post',
            name='author',

field=models.CharField(max_length=100),
        ),
    ]
```

In this example:

- The `AddField` operation reflects the change you made to the `Post` model (adding the `author` field).
- The `dependencies` section ensures that migrations are applied in the correct order.

2. Applying Migrations

Once migrations are created, you can apply them to the database to update the schema. This is done with the `migrate` command:

```bash
bash
```

```bash
python manage.py migrate
```

This command looks at the migration files and applies them to the database. It will only apply migrations that haven't been run yet, ensuring that your database is always in sync with your models.

- **Step 1: Check the Status of Migrations**

If you want to check which migrations have been applied and which are pending, you can use the following command:

```bash
bash
```

```bash
python manage.py showmigrations
```

This will display a list of migrations for each app, with an X next to the ones that have been applied and an empty box next to the ones that haven't.

- **Step 2: Apply All Pending Migrations**

To apply all pending migrations for your project, simply run:

bash

```
python manage.py migrate
```

- **Step 3: Apply Migrations for a Specific App**

If you want to apply migrations for a specific app, you can specify the app name:

bash

```
python manage.py migrate your_app_name
```

3. Rolling Back Migrations

In some cases, you might need to undo migrations. Django allows you to roll back migrations using the `migrate` command by specifying a migration to revert to.

To undo a migration and roll back to the previous state, use:

bash

170

```
python manage.py migrate your_app_name 0001
```

This will revert the `your_app_name` app back to the state of the `0001` migration.

4. Making and Applying Migrations for Multiple Apps

If you want to create and apply migrations for all apps in your project at once, you can run:

```bash
bash

python manage.py makemigrations
python manage.py migrate
```

Best Practices for Managing Migrations

Managing migrations effectively is important to ensure that your database schema remains consistent across environments, and migrations are applied smoothly. Here are some best practices for managing migrations:

1. Keep Migrations in Version Control

Always commit your migration files to your version control system (e.g., Git). This ensures that everyone working on the project has the same migration files, and migrations can be easily applied across different environments (development, staging, production).

2. Use Descriptive Migration Names

When generating migrations, try to give them descriptive names that indicate the purpose of the migration. For example:

```bash
python manage.py makemigrations your_app_name --
name add_author_field_to_post
```

This will generate a migration with a name like 0002_add_author_field_to_post.py, which makes it easier to understand the purpose of the migration.

3. Avoid Making Large, Complex Migrations

Large migrations that include multiple schema changes (e.g., adding many fields or tables in one migration) can be difficult to manage and review. Instead, try to create smaller, focused migrations that represent one logical change at a time.

4. Test Migrations Locally

Before applying migrations in a production environment, always test them locally or on a staging server. This helps ensure that the migrations work correctly and don't introduce errors that could break your application.

5. Avoid Directly Editing Migration Files

While it's possible to manually edit migration files, it's best to avoid doing so unless absolutely necessary. Django's migration system is designed to work automatically, and manually editing migrations can lead to issues, especially when working in teams.

If you need to change a model after it has already been migrated, it's generally better to create a new migration rather than editing the old one.

6. Use `migrate --plan` for Previewing Changes

Before applying migrations, you can use the `--plan` flag to preview what changes will be made to the database:

```bash
python manage.py migrate --plan
```

This shows what migrations will be applied, so you can review them before actually making changes to the database.

7. Handling Conflicts in Migrations

If you work with a team, you might encounter **migration conflicts** if two people create migrations that modify the same part of the schema. If this happens, Django will ask you to resolve the conflict manually by merging the migration files.

To handle conflicts, run:

```bash
bash
```

```
python manage.py makemigrations your_app_name
```

If Django detects a conflict, it will prompt you to merge the conflicting migrations. You can manually edit the migration files to resolve the conflict, or Django might automatically resolve the issue if the changes are simple.

8. Use Data Migrations for Non-Schema Changes

Sometimes, migrations need to change data (e.g., populating a new field with values or modifying the data in an existing field). Django supports **data migrations** that can be used for these kinds of operations.

- **Example of a Data Migration**:

```python
python

from django.db import migrations

def populate_author(apps, schema_editor):
    Post   =   apps.get_model('your_app_name',
'Post')
    for post in Post.objects.all():
        post.author = 'Unknown'
        post.save()
```

174

```
class Migration(migrations.Migration):
    dependencies = [
        ('your_app_name',
'0002_add_author_field_to_post'),
    ]

    operations = [
        migrations.RunPython(populate_author),
    ]
```

This migration adds an `author` field to the `Post` model and then uses the `RunPython` operation to populate the `author` field with a default value for all existing records.

Summary

In this chapter, we covered **database migrations** in Django and how they allow you to manage changes to your database schema in a structured and versioned manner. We walked through how to create and apply migrations, roll back migrations, and best practices for managing migrations effectively. Using Django's migration system ensures that your database schema evolves safely and consistently as your application grows.

By following best practices such as keeping migrations in version control, testing them locally, and avoiding large complex migrations, you can maintain a clean and manageable database schema throughout the life of your project.

CHAPTER 17

ADVANCED DJANGO MODELS AND RELATIONSHIPS

Django's ORM provides powerful tools to define and manage relationships between models. Understanding how to handle complex relationships is key to building robust applications with Django. In this chapter, we'll explore how to manage **one-to-many**, **many-to-many**, and **one-to-one** relationships using Django's `ForeignKey`, `ManyToManyField`, and `OneToOneField`. We'll also dive into how to optimize database queries using `select_related` and `prefetch_related` to improve performance when working with related models.

Handling Complex Relationships (One-to-Many, Many-to-Many)

Django models can have complex relationships between them, and Django provides different field types to handle these relationships. Let's break down each type of relationship and how to implement them.

1. One-to-Many Relationship

176

A **one-to-many relationship** is when one model can be related to many instances of another model. In Django, this is implemented using a `ForeignKey`.

Example: One-to-Many with `ForeignKey`

Consider a blog application where a `Post` can have multiple `Comment`s. Each comment belongs to exactly one post, which represents a **one-to-many** relationship.

```python
from django.db import models

class Post(models.Model):
    title = models.CharField(max_length=100)
    content = models.TextField()
    published_date                          =
models.DateTimeField(auto_now_add=True)

    def __str__(self):
        return self.title

class Comment(models.Model):
    post          =          models.ForeignKey(Post,
on_delete=models.CASCADE,
related_name='comments')
    text = models.TextField()
```

```
created_at                                    =
models.DateTimeField(auto_now_add=True)

    def __str__(self):
        return f"Comment on {self.post.title}"
```

In this example:

- `ForeignKey` creates the one-to-many relationship: Each `Comment` belongs to a single `Post`, but a `Post` can have multiple `Comments`.
- `on_delete=models.CASCADE`: When a `Post` is deleted, all associated comments are deleted as well.
- `related_name='comments'`: This specifies the reverse relationship, so you can access all comments for a post with `post.comments.all()`.

2. Many-to-Many Relationship

A **many-to-many relationship** is when multiple instances of one model can be related to multiple instances of another model. This is implemented in Django using the `ManyToManyField`.

Example: Many-to-Many with `ManyToManyField`

In a book application, a `Book` can have multiple `Authors`, and an `Author` can write multiple `Books`. This is a **many-to-many** relationship.

```python
python

class Author(models.Model):
    name = models.CharField(max_length=100)
    birthdate = models.DateField()

    def __str__(self):
        return self.name

class Book(models.Model):
    title = models.CharField(max_length=200)
    authors  =  models.ManyToManyField(Author,
related_name='books')
    published_date = models.DateTimeField()

    def __str__(self):
        return self.title
```

In this example:

- `ManyToManyField` creates the many-to-many relationship: Each `Book` can have multiple `Author`s, and each `Author` can be associated with multiple `Book`s.
- `related_name='books'`: This allows you to access all books written by an author with `author.books.all()`.

3. One-to-One Relationship

A **one-to-one relationship** is when each instance of a model is related to exactly one instance of another model. This is implemented using `OneToOneField`.

Example: One-to-One with `OneToOneField`

Let's assume that each `UserProfile` is linked to exactly one `User` in your Django application. This represents a **one-to-one** relationship.

python

```python
from django.contrib.auth.models import User

class UserProfile(models.Model):
    user        =        models.OneToOneField(User,
on_delete=models.CASCADE,
related_name='profile')
    bio = models.TextField()
    website = models.URLField()

    def __str__(self):
        return        f"Profile        for
{self.user.username}"
```

In this example:

- `OneToOneField` creates the one-to-one relationship: Each `UserProfile` is linked to a single `User`.

- `related_name='profile'`: This allows you to access the user profile from the user model using `user.profile`.

Optimizing Queries with `select_related` and `prefetch_related`

Django provides two powerful query optimization techniques—`select_related` and `prefetch_related`—to reduce the number of queries executed when working with related objects. These methods help in improving the performance of database queries, especially when dealing with foreign key and many-to-many relationships.

1. `select_related` (For One-to-Many and One-to-One Relationships)

`select_related` is used for **forward relationships** (i.e., `ForeignKey` and `OneToOneField`). It performs a SQL **JOIN** and retrieves related objects in a single query, which is much more efficient than querying the related objects separately.

Example: Using `select_related`

Consider a `Comment` model with a `ForeignKey` to `Post`. Without `select_related`, Django would execute a separate query for each `Comment` when accessing its associated `Post`.

181

```python
python

# Without select_related
comments = Comment.objects.all()
for comment in comments:
    print(comment.post.title)   # Each access to
`comment.post` triggers a new query
```

By using `select_related`, we can optimize the query to fetch the `Post` objects in the same query as the `Comment` objects.

```python
python

# With select_related
comments                                    =
Comment.objects.select_related('post').all()
for comment in comments:
    print(comment.post.title)   # No additional
queries are triggered
```

In this example:

- `select_related('post')` fetches the `Post` associated with each `Comment` in a single query using a SQL JOIN.
- This reduces the number of queries and improves performance when accessing related data.

182

2. `prefetch_related` (For Many-to-Many and Reverse Relationships)

`prefetch_related` is used for **many-to-many** relationships and **reverse foreign key** relationships (i.e., when you want to access the related objects from the other side of a relationship). Unlike `select_related`, which performs a JOIN, `prefetch_related` performs a separate query for each related model and then combines them in Python.

Example: Using `prefetch_related`

If you have a `Book` model with a many-to-many relationship with `Author`, querying all `Books` and accessing their authors could result in multiple queries. We can optimize this by using `prefetch_related`.

python

```
# Without prefetch_related
books = Book.objects.all()
for book in books:
    print(book.authors.all())   # Each access to
`book.authors` triggers a new query
```

Using `prefetch_related`, we can reduce the number of queries.

```python
python
```

```python
# With prefetch_related
books                                          =
Book.objects.prefetch_related('authors').all()
for book in books:
    print(book.authors.all())  # Only two queries
are executed (one for books, one for authors)
```

In this example:

- `prefetch_related('authors')` fetches all authors for the books in a separate query and caches the results. This allows for faster access to the related `authors` without triggering additional queries.

3. Combining `select_related` and `prefetch_related`

You can combine `select_related` and `prefetch_related` to optimize queries when dealing with both **one-to-many** and **many-to-many** relationships.

Example: Combining Both:

```python
python
```

```python
# Efficient query with select_related for
ForeignKey and prefetch_related for ManyToMany
```

```
books                                    =
Book.objects.select_related('publisher').prefet
ch_related('authors').all()
for book in books:
    print(book.publisher.name)
    print([author.name    for    author    in
book.authors.all()])
```

In this example:

- `select_related('publisher')` efficiently fetches the related publisher using a JOIN.
- `prefetch_related('authors')` fetches all authors related to the books using a separate query and caches them.

Best Practices for Managing Relationships and Optimizing Queries

1. **Use `select_related` for Single-Value Relationships**: If you're working with `ForeignKey` or `OneToOneField` relationships, always use `select_related` to reduce the number of queries and optimize performance.

2. **Use `prefetch_related` for Multi-Value Relationships**: When dealing with `ManyToManyField` or reverse relationships (i.e., when accessing related objects from the other side of the relationship), use `prefetch_related` to perform efficient queries.

3. **Avoid N+1 Query Problems**: One of the most common performance issues when working with Django ORM is the N+1 query problem, where accessing related objects triggers a separate query for each object. Use `select_related` and `prefetch_related` to avoid this problem and optimize query performance.

4. **Use `only()` and `defer()` to Optimize Field Access**: If you don't need all the fields in a model, you can use the `only()` or `defer()` methods to limit the fields that are fetched from the database. This can improve performance by reducing the amount of data retrieved.

5. **Test Query Performance**: Use Django's `django.db.connection.queries` to monitor and test the number of queries your application is making. This helps you spot inefficiencies and optimize queries before they become performance bottlenecks.

Summary

In this chapter, we covered **advanced relationships** in Django, including **one-to-many**, **many-to-many**, and **one-to-one** relationships, and how to manage them using `ForeignKey`, `ManyToManyField`, and `OneToOneField`. We also explored **query optimization techniques** using `select_related` and `prefetch_related` to reduce the number of queries executed and improve the performance of your application.

186

Understanding and optimizing Django's ORM relationships is crucial for building efficient, scalable applications. By applying these techniques, you can ensure your Django application runs efficiently, even as it grows and handles complex data models.

CHAPTER 18

WORKING WITH DJANGO'S MIDDLEWARE

Middleware is a core concept in Django that allows you to process requests globally before they reach the view or after the view has processed them. Middleware provides hooks for processing the request and response cycle, making it a powerful tool for various tasks, such as authentication, session handling, logging, and modifying the response.

In this chapter, we will dive into what middleware is, how it works in Django, and how to customize and use middleware for different purposes.

Introduction to Middleware

Middleware is a lightweight, low-level plugin system for globally altering Django's input or output. It is a framework of hooks into Django's request/response processing. Each middleware component is instantiated once and processes each request as it comes in. Similarly, middleware components are executed when sending a response back to the client.

Middleware is usually used for:

- Request and response processing.

- Session handling.

- User authentication and permissions checking.

- CSRF protection and security headers.

- Request logging and performance monitoring.

- Modifying or logging the HTTP request and response objects.

Django processes requests in the following order:

1. **Request Handling**: The request is passed through each middleware (in order) before it reaches the view.

2. **View Handling**: Once the request has passed through middleware, Django processes the view logic and generates the response.

3. **Response Handling**: The response is passed back through the middleware (in reverse order) before being sent to the client.

How Middleware Works in Django

Django's middleware is executed during the request-response cycle, as described above. Middleware classes are executed in the order they are defined in the `MIDDLEWARE` setting in the `settings.py` file. Django executes middleware functions both on requests and responses.

1. Middleware in Django Settings

To enable middleware, you need to add it to the MIDDLEWARE setting in your settings.py file. This setting contains a list of middleware classes that Django will run during the request and response cycle.

For example:

```python

MIDDLEWARE = [

'django.middleware.security.SecurityMiddleware'
,

'django.contrib.sessions.middleware.SessionMidd
leware',

'django.middleware.common.CommonMiddleware',

'django.middleware.csrf.CsrfViewMiddleware',

'django.contrib.auth.middleware.AuthenticationM
iddleware',

'django.contrib.messages.middleware.MessageMidd
leware',

'django.middleware.clickjacking.XFrameOptionsMi
ddleware',
```

]

- Each string in the list represents a middleware class, and these classes are executed in the order they are listed.
- The `MIDDLEWARE` setting is predefined by Django with common middleware components like `SessionMiddleware`, `AuthenticationMiddleware`, and `CommonMiddleware`. These are responsible for handling requests, managing sessions, processing CSRF tokens, etc.

2. Request-Processing Middleware

Request-processing middleware is called on every request before it is passed to the view. This middleware can perform tasks such as:

- Modifying the request object.
- Processing user authentication.
- Checking user permissions.
- Logging requests for monitoring purposes.

Example of Request-Processing Middleware:

```python
from datetime import datetime
```

```
class TimeLoggingMiddleware:
    def __init__(self, get_response):
        self.get_response = get_response

    def __call__(self, request):
        print(f"Request         received         at:
{datetime.now()}")
        response = self.get_response(request)
        return response
```

In this example:

- The __init__ method receives the get_response function, which will be called later in the middleware chain.
- The __call__ method is invoked on each request, allowing you to modify or log the request before passing it to the next middleware or view.

3. Response-Processing Middleware

Response-processing middleware is called after the view has processed the request and returned a response. It is responsible for modifying the response before it is sent to the client. Common use cases for response-processing middleware include:

- Adding custom headers to the response.
- Modifying the content of the response.

- Handling response caching or compression.

Example of Response-Processing Middleware:

python

```python
class AddHeaderMiddleware:
    def __init__(self, get_response):
        self.get_response = get_response

    def __call__(self, request):
        response = self.get_response(request)
        response['X-Custom-Header']  =  'Hello,
World!'  # Adding a custom header to the response
        return response
```

In this example:

- After the view processes the request and generates a response, the AddHeaderMiddleware adds a custom header (X-Custom-Header) to the response.

Customizing and Using Middleware for Different Purposes

Django allows you to create custom middleware to handle specific tasks or modify requests and responses in a way that is tailored to your application.

1. Writing Custom Middleware

193

To create custom middleware, you need to define a class with an __init__ method and a __call__ method (as shown above). The __call__ method will handle the request and response. You can also choose to implement methods like process_request or process_response (if you're working with older versions of Django, but these are now deprecated).

Here's a more detailed example of a custom middleware that handles authentication:

python

```python
from django.http import HttpResponseForbidden

class AuthMiddleware:
    def __init__(self, get_response):
        self.get_response = get_response

    def __call__(self, request):
        if not request.user.is_authenticated:
            return    HttpResponseForbidden("You
must be logged in to view this page.")
        response = self.get_response(request)
        return response
```

In this example:

- If the user is not authenticated (request.user.is_authenticated), the

194

middleware prevents further processing by returning a `403 Forbidden` response.

- If the user is authenticated, the request continues, and the response is generated by the view.

2. Ordering Middleware

The order in which middleware is listed in the `MIDDLEWARE` setting is crucial because middleware processes requests and responses in the order they are listed. For example:

- Authentication middleware (e.g., `AuthenticationMiddleware`) should be placed before any middleware that depends on the user being authenticated.
- CSRF protection middleware (e.g., `CsrfViewMiddleware`) should be placed before any middleware that handles form submissions.

3. Middleware for Caching

Middleware can also be used to manage caching of views or static files. Django provides a built-in `CacheMiddleware` that caches the output of views. You can use it to improve performance by caching responses based on the request URL.

Example: Enabling Cache Middleware

```python
python

MIDDLEWARE = [

'django.middleware.cache.UpdateCacheMiddleware'
,  # Updates the cache on every request

'django.middleware.cache.FetchFromCacheMiddlewa
re',  # Fetches the response from cache
]
```

This middleware ensures that responses are cached and reused for subsequent requests, improving performance.

4. Middleware for Handling Security

Django provides several middleware classes that help handle common security concerns:

- **SecurityMiddleware**: Adds HTTP headers to help protect against security vulnerabilities, such as clickjacking, cross-site scripting (XSS), and SSL hijacking.
- **XFrameOptionsMiddleware**: Prevents your site from being embedded in an iframe, protecting against clickjacking attacks.

- **CsrfViewMiddleware**: Provides protection against Cross-Site Request Forgery (CSRF) attacks by validating the CSRF token.

You can add these middleware classes to your project's MIDDLEWARE setting for enhanced security.

5. Middleware for Request Logging

You can create custom middleware to log incoming requests or monitor application performance.

Example: Logging Request Information

```python
import logging

class RequestLoggingMiddleware:
    def __init__(self, get_response):
        self.get_response = get_response
        self.logger              =
logging.getLogger(__name__)

    def __call__(self, request):
        self.logger.info(f"Request    made    to
{request.path}                           from
{request.META.get('REMOTE_ADDR')}")
        response = self.get_response(request)
```

```
return response
```

This middleware logs each request made to the server, along with the request path and the client's IP address.

Best Practices for Middleware

1. **Keep Middleware Lightweight**: Middleware should only perform lightweight operations, as they are executed on every request. Avoid putting complex logic that may impact performance.

2. **Order Middleware Properly**: Be mindful of the order of middleware. For example, `AuthenticationMiddleware` should come before any middleware that relies on user authentication.

3. **Use Built-in Middleware When Possible**: Django provides a variety of built-in middleware to handle common tasks (e.g., security, caching, session management). Use these before writing custom middleware.

4. **Ensure Middleware Does Not Overlap**: Avoid creating middleware that performs the same task as built-in middleware (e.g., authentication or session handling) unless you have a specific need.

5. **Test Middleware**: Ensure that your custom middleware works correctly by testing it with different request types, users, and response scenarios.

Summary

In this chapter, we explored **middleware** in Django, which is a powerful tool for modifying the request and response cycle globally. We covered how middleware works, the types of tasks middleware can handle, and how to create and customize middleware to meet the needs of your application. Middleware is essential for managing tasks like authentication, security, caching, and logging, and is an integral part of Django's request/response architecture.

By understanding how to write and use middleware effectively, you can add functionality to your Django application that operates consistently across the entire request/response cycle.

CHAPTER 19

DJANGO TESTING – ENSURING CODE QUALITY

Testing is a crucial part of software development, ensuring that your code behaves as expected and preventing bugs from reaching production. Django comes with a built-in testing framework that allows you to write unit tests and integration tests to validate the functionality of your application. In this chapter, we'll explore how to write and run tests in Django, how to write both unit tests and integration tests, and how to improve test coverage for better code quality.

Introduction to Testing in Django

Testing in Django is built around Python's `unittest` module, with Django providing additional test utilities to help you work with the framework's components. Django tests are designed to be simple, and the framework provides tools for testing models, views, forms, templates, and more.

Django comes with the following key features for testing:

- **Test case classes**: `TestCase` classes extend Django's `unittest.TestCase` and provide extra functionality for testing Django-specific features.
- **Database setup**: Django provides a test database, so tests run in an isolated environment, allowing you to test without affecting the production data.
- **Test clients**: Django includes a test client for simulating HTTP requests and interacting with your views.
- **Assertions**: Django provides several assertions to test responses, templates, database queries, and more.

Writing tests helps ensure that your application remains reliable, and it allows you to catch potential issues early in the development process. Tests also act as documentation, providing clear examples of how your application should behave.

Writing Unit Tests and Integration Tests

1. Writing Unit Tests

Unit tests focus on testing small, isolated pieces of functionality in your application, such as individual functions or methods. They are the simplest form of testing and usually don't require external resources like databases or APIs.

Example: Testing a Model Method

Consider a `Post` model with a method to retrieve the first 100 characters of the post's content.

python

```python
from django.db import models

class Post(models.Model):
    title = models.CharField(max_length=100)
    content = models.TextField()

    def get_excerpt(self):
        return self.content[:100]
```

You can write a unit test for the `get_excerpt` method to ensure that it returns the expected result:

python

```python
from django.test import TestCase
from .models import Post

class PostModelTest(TestCase):
    def test_get_excerpt(self):
        # Create a Post object
        post = Post.objects.create(title="Test Post", content="This is a sample post content that is longer than 100 characters.")
```

```
# Test the get_excerpt method
self.assertEqual(post.get_excerpt(),
"This is a sample post content that is longer
than 100 characters.")
```

In this test:

- The `test_get_excerpt` method creates a `Post` object with some content and checks if `get_excerpt()` returns the correct first 100 characters.

2. Writing Integration Tests

Integration tests are broader tests that validate the interaction between different parts of your application, such as views, forms, and models. These tests ensure that your application works as expected when all components are combined.

Example: Testing a View

Let's say you have a view that lists all `Post` objects. You can write an integration test to ensure that this view correctly renders the list of posts.

```python
python

from django.test import TestCase
from django.urls import reverse
from .models import Post
```

```
class PostViewTest(TestCase):
    def test_post_list_view(self):
        # Create a few Post objects
        post1 = Post.objects.create(title="Post
1", content="Content of post 1")
        post2 = Post.objects.create(title="Post
2", content="Content of post 2")

        # Send a GET request to the post list
view
        response                              =
self.client.get(reverse('post_list'))          #
Assuming the view URL is named 'post_list'

        # Check that the response is 200 OK and
that the posts are rendered
        self.assertEqual(response.status_code,
200)
        self.assertContains(response, "Post 1")
        self.assertContains(response, "Post 2")
```

In this test:

- We create two `Post` objects and send a GET request to the `post_list` view.
- The test checks if the response status is `200 OK` and whether the post titles are included in the rendered HTML.

3. Testing Forms

You can also test Django forms to ensure they handle data correctly.

Example: Testing a Form

Consider a form for creating `Post` objects:

python

```python
from django import forms
from .models import Post

class PostForm(forms.ModelForm):
    class Meta:
        model = Post
        fields = ['title', 'content']
```

Here's a test that validates the form:

python

```python
from django.test import TestCase
from .forms import PostForm

class PostFormTest(TestCase):
    def test_valid_form(self):
        form_data = {'title': 'Test Post',
'content': 'This is a valid post content.'}
```

```
        form = PostForm(data=form_data)
        self.assertTrue(form.is_valid())

    def test_invalid_form(self):
        form_data = {'title': '', 'content':
'Content without a title.'}
        form = PostForm(data=form_data)
        self.assertFalse(form.is_valid())
```

In this test:

- The `test_valid_form` method checks that a valid form submission is considered valid.
- The `test_invalid_form` method checks that an invalid form (missing title) is correctly marked as invalid.

Running Tests and Improving Test Coverage

1. Running Tests

Django provides a built-in test runner that helps you run your tests and see the results. To run your tests, use the following command:

```bash
bash
```

```
python manage.py test
```

Django will discover and run all the tests in your project (in any file starting with `test_`), displaying the results in the terminal.

- **Running Tests for a Specific App**: To run tests for a specific app, specify the app name:

bash

```
python manage.py test your_app_name
```

- **Running Tests for a Specific Test Case or Method**: You can also specify a particular test case or method to run:

bash

```
python          manage.py          test
your_app_name.tests.test_file.TestCaseNam
e
```

2. Improving Test Coverage

Test coverage measures how much of your code is covered by tests. To improve coverage, ensure that you test the most important parts of your application, such as:

- Views, especially for critical functionality like authentication, data display, and form submissions.
- Models, especially custom methods and database interactions.
- Forms and validation logic.
- Error handling, ensuring that your app behaves correctly in edge cases.

Some tips to improve test coverage:

- **Test Edge Cases**: Test for edge cases and unexpected inputs (e.g., empty fields, large data sets).
- **Test All View Logic**: Ensure that each view, especially those with forms or business logic, is thoroughly tested for both valid and invalid inputs.
- **Use Mocking**: For external APIs or services, use **mocking** to simulate their behavior during testing.
- **Measure Coverage**: You can use tools like `coverage.py` to measure how much of your code is covered by tests.

3. Best Practices for Testing in Django

- **Write Tests as You Develop**: Writing tests as you develop new features ensures that your code is tested and catches issues early.
- **Isolate Tests**: Ensure your tests are isolated. Each test should run independently, meaning it should not depend on the success of other tests.
- **Use Django's Test Client**: Django provides a test client (`self.client`) that simulates HTTP requests and lets you test your views and responses without needing an actual browser.

- **Test with Different User Scenarios**: Test different user roles and permissions to ensure your app behaves correctly for different users.

- **Use Fixtures**: Django supports test fixtures, allowing you to load initial data into the database for tests. This is useful for testing with pre-existing data.

- **Automate Tests**: Automate running tests as part of your development workflow, such as using continuous integration tools like GitHub Actions or Travis CI.

Summary

In this chapter, we covered how to use Django's testing framework to write unit and integration tests. We explored how to test models, views, forms, and ensure that your application behaves as expected. We also discussed how to run tests, improve test coverage, and follow best practices to maintain code quality. Testing is a fundamental practice for building reliable and maintainable Django applications, and following these guidelines will help ensure that your code remains robust and free of bugs.

CHAPTER 20

DEBUGGING AND TROUBLESHOOTING IN DJANGO

Debugging is an essential skill for any developer. In this chapter, we will explore common errors you might encounter while developing with Django, how to troubleshoot these issues, and how to use Django's built-in debugging tools to help identify and fix problems. We'll also discuss debugging workflows and best practices to streamline the debugging process and make your development more efficient.

Common Errors and How to Troubleshoot Them

Django applications can encounter a variety of errors, ranging from simple mistakes in code to more complex issues related to configuration or dependencies. Here are some of the most common types of errors in Django and tips on how to troubleshoot them:

1. `ImproperlyConfigured` Errors

- **Description**: This error occurs when Django cannot find or properly configure a setting or dependency.
- **Example**:

```
python
```

```
ImproperlyConfigured: You're using the
`django.contrib.sessions.middleware.Sessi
onMiddleware` middleware, but the
`SESSION_ENGINE` setting is missing.
```

- **Solution**: Ensure that all required settings are defined in your `settings.py` file, such as database configurations, middleware settings, and installed apps.

2. `DoesNotExist` Error

- **Description**: This error occurs when a query does not return any results, typically when trying to fetch an object from the database that doesn't exist.

- **Example**:

```
python
```

```
Post.DoesNotExist: Post matching query
does not exist.
```

- **Solution**: Ensure that your database contains the necessary data. You can also use `get_object_or_404()` instead of `get()` to return a 404 error if the object doesn't exist, preventing the `DoesNotExist` error.

```python
```

```
from        django.shortcuts        import
get_object_or_404
post = get_object_or_404(Post, pk=post_id)
```

3. TemplateDoesNotExist Error

- **Description**: This error occurs when Django cannot find the template file specified in your view.
- **Example**:

```python
```

```
TemplateDoesNotExist: my_template.html
```

- **Solution**: Check that the template is located in one of the directories listed in the TEMPLATES setting in your settings.py file. Ensure that the template filename is spelled correctly and exists in the correct location.

4. OperationalError (Database Connection Errors)

- **Description**: This error occurs when there's an issue with your database connection, such as incorrect credentials, a missing database, or a database that is down.
- **Example**:

```python
```

```
OperationalError: (1045, "Access denied
for user 'myuser'@'localhost' (using
password: YES)")
```

- **Solution**: Check your database settings in `settings.py`, ensure that the database server is running, and verify that the user credentials and database name are correct. Additionally, confirm that the database is accessible from your Django app.

5. `ValidationError` in Forms

- **Description**: This error occurs when form validation fails, usually because the data submitted does not meet the requirements defined in the form fields.
- **Example**:

```python
python

ValidationError: ['This field is
required.']
```

- **Solution**: Review the form validation logic and ensure that the submitted data meets all validation criteria. Check the form's fields for constraints such as `required`, `max_length`, or custom validation.

6. 500 Internal Server Error

213

- **Description**: A generic error indicating that something went wrong on the server-side.
- **Solution**: To get more information about the error, check the error logs. In development mode, Django displays detailed error pages that include tracebacks, which can help identify the source of the error.

Using Django's Built-in Debugging Tools

Django provides several built-in debugging tools that can help you identify issues during development. These tools allow you to view detailed error messages, inspect the code's execution, and interact with the application in a more productive way.

1. Django Debug Mode

When `DEBUG` is set to `True` in your `settings.py`, Django displays detailed error pages when an error occurs during a request. These pages include:

- The exception traceback.
- The context of the error, such as the request method, request path, and user information.
- The values of local variables in the view function where the error occurred.

Example: Enabling Debug Mode

```python
```

```
# settings.py
DEBUG = True
```

With `DEBUG = True`, Django will show detailed error pages for unhandled exceptions, helping you identify issues quickly.

2. The Django Debug Toolbar

The **Django Debug Toolbar** is a popular third-party package that provides a set of panels displaying various debugging information about the request-response cycle, such as:

- SQL queries made by Django ORM.
- Template rendering time.
- Cache usage.
- Request headers and data.
- Session and cookie information.

To install and configure the Django Debug Toolbar:

```bash
```

```
pip install django-debug-toolbar
```

Then, add it to your `INSTALLED_APPS` and middleware:

```python
```

```
# settings.py
INSTALLED_APPS = [
    # Other apps...
    'debug_toolbar',
]

MIDDLEWARE = [
    # Other middleware...

'debug_toolbar.middleware.DebugToolbarMiddlewar
e',
]

INTERNAL_IPS = ['127.0.0.1']  # Required for the
Debug Toolbar to display
```

Once configured, the toolbar will appear on your web pages, providing a wealth of diagnostic information.

3. Logging with Django

Django includes a robust logging framework that you can use to track application behavior and errors. You can configure different loggers to capture information at various levels (e.g., debug, info, warning, error, critical).

Example: Configuring Logging in `settings.py`

```python
python

LOGGING = {
    'version': 1,
    'disable_existing_loggers': False,
    'handlers': {
        'file': {
            'level': 'ERROR',
            'class': 'logging.FileHandler',
            'filename': 'errors.log',
        },
    },
    'loggers': {
        'django': {
            'handlers': ['file'],
            'level': 'ERROR',
            'propagate': True,
        },
    },
}
```

This configuration sends error-level logs to a file (`errors.log`). You can adjust the logging level based on the severity of the issues you want to track.

4. Django Shell for Interactive Debugging

Django's **shell** provides an interactive Python environment where you can inspect and manipulate your models, query the database,

217

and execute code to troubleshoot issues. You can use the Django shell to interact with your application in real-time.

To enter the shell:

```bash
python manage.py shell
```

Once inside, you can execute Python commands and experiment with your Django models and views:

```python
from myapp.models import Post
post = Post.objects.first()
print(post.title)
```

Debugging Workflows and Best Practices

While debugging, it's important to have a systematic approach to troubleshooting issues. Here are some tips and best practices to enhance your debugging workflow:

1. Reproduce the Issue Locally

Before trying to fix the issue, reproduce it in a local development environment. Ensure you can replicate the error consistently to understand its cause.

2. Use the Django Debugger (pdb)

You can use Python's built-in debugger, pdb, to step through your code line by line, inspect variables, and see where things go wrong.

Example of using pdb:

```python
import pdb

def my_view(request):
    pdb.set_trace()   # Program will pause here and open the interactive debugger
    # Your view logic here
```

Once pdb.set_trace() is hit, the debugger will pause, and you can inspect variables and navigate through the code.

3. Check Logs Regularly

Always check your logs for errors. Logs can provide additional context when an issue arises and help you pinpoint the cause of the error.

4. Test Changes and Revert if Necessary

When you make changes to fix an issue, run your tests to ensure the application is still functioning correctly. If the problem persists or the fix introduces new issues, be prepared to revert changes or debug further.

5. Use Version Control (Git) for Debugging

If you are working in a team, always commit your changes regularly. Use Git branches to isolate work and help avoid overwriting each other's changes. If you suspect an error is related to recent changes, use `git bisect` to identify the commit where the issue was introduced.

6. Isolate Issues to Specific Areas

Break down the issue and narrow it down to a specific part of the application (e.g., models, views, templates). Use Django's built-in testing and logging features to gain insights and isolate the root cause.

7. Take Breaks

If you're stuck on an issue, take a break. Sometimes stepping away from the problem for a few minutes or hours can help you see it from a fresh perspective and lead to new insights.

Summary

In this chapter, we discussed how to handle debugging and troubleshooting in Django. We covered common errors you may encounter, how to troubleshoot them, and the built-in tools Django provides for debugging, including the Django Debug Toolbar, logging, and the Django shell. Additionally, we explored best practices for debugging workflows, such as reproducing issues locally, using pdb for stepping through code, and checking logs regularly.

By using Django's debugging tools and following a systematic debugging process, you can quickly identify and fix issues, ensuring your application runs smoothly and is of high quality.

CHAPTER 21

DJANGO DEPLOYMENT – FROM LOCAL TO LIVE

Deploying a Django application from a local development environment to a production server involves several important steps, including configuring settings, using a production-ready server, and securing your application. This chapter will guide you through the process of preparing your Django project for production, deploying it with WSGI and Gunicorn, and configuring a production database and environment.

Preparing Your Django Project for Production

Before you deploy your Django application, there are several essential steps to ensure it runs smoothly and securely in a production environment.

1. Set DEBUG to False

In development, Django's DEBUG setting is set to True, which gives detailed error pages and enables other development features. In production, this should be set to False for security reasons, as showing detailed error pages can expose sensitive information about your application.

```python
python
```

```python
# settings.py
DEBUG = False
```

2. Configure Allowed Hosts

The ALLOWED_HOSTS setting defines the domain names and IP addresses that your Django site can serve. This prevents HTTP Host header attacks by ensuring that Django only responds to requests from trusted hosts.

```python
python
```

```python
# settings.py
ALLOWED_HOSTS           =           ['yourdomain.com',
'www.yourdomain.com', 'localhost']
```

3. Use Environment Variables for Sensitive Information

Do not store sensitive information like database passwords, secret keys, or API keys directly in your settings.py file. Instead, use environment variables or a .env file to manage sensitive information securely.

You can use the **python-dotenv** library to load environment variables from a .env file:

```bash
bash
```

223

```
pip install python-dotenv
```

Then, in your `settings.py`, load the environment variables:

```python
python

from dotenv import load_dotenv
import os

load_dotenv()

SECRET_KEY = os.getenv('DJANGO_SECRET_KEY')
DATABASE_PASSWORD                              =
os.getenv('DATABASE_PASSWORD')
```

In your `.env` file, store the sensitive values:

```text
text

DJANGO_SECRET_KEY=your_secret_key
DATABASE_PASSWORD=your_database_password
```

4. Static and Media Files Configuration

In production, you'll need to configure Django to serve static files (CSS, JavaScript, images) and media files (uploads). Use `django-storages` or a similar tool for handling static and media files on cloud services like AWS, or configure Nginx to serve them directly.

224

For example, set up `STATIC_ROOT` and `MEDIA_ROOT` in `settings.py`:

python

```
# settings.py
STATIC_ROOT = os.path.join(BASE_DIR, 'static')
MEDIA_ROOT = os.path.join(BASE_DIR, 'media')

# The URL at which static and media files will be
served
STATIC_URL = '/static/'
MEDIA_URL = '/media/'
```

Run `collectstatic` to gather all static files into the `STATIC_ROOT` directory:

bash

```
python manage.py collectstatic
```

5. Set Up Logging

In production, it's important to have proper logging to monitor errors and application behavior. Django's logging system can log errors, warnings, and other events to files, databases, or external services.

Here's an example of logging configuration for production:

225

```python
python

# settings.py
LOGGING = {
    'version': 1,
    'disable_existing_loggers': False,
    'handlers': {
        'file': {
            'level': 'ERROR',
            'class': 'logging.FileHandler',
            'filename': 'django_errors.log',
        },
    },
    'loggers': {
        'django': {
            'handlers': ['file'],
            'level': 'ERROR',
            'propagate': True,
        },
    },
}
```

This configuration logs all error-level messages and above to the django_errors.log file.

Deploying Django with WSGI and Gunicorn

For a production environment, you need a production-ready WSGI (Web Server Gateway Interface) server. Gunicorn is one of the most popular WSGI servers for Django applications, and it serves as a bridge between Django and your web server (e.g., Nginx or Apache).

1. Install Gunicorn

First, install Gunicorn in your environment:

bash

```
pip install gunicorn
```

2. Running Gunicorn

Run Gunicorn as the WSGI server for your Django application. From the root of your Django project, run:

bash

```
gunicorn --workers 3 myproject.wsgi:application
```

- `--workers 3`: Specifies the number of worker processes. The number of workers should be roughly equal to $(2 \times NUM\_CORES) + 1$ for optimal performance.
- `myproject.wsgi:application`: This points to the WSGI application in your project, which is typically located in the `wsgi.py` file of your Django project.

Gunicorn will start the server, and you can access your Django application by navigating to the appropriate address (e.g., `http://127.0.0.1:8000`).

3. Running Gunicorn in Production

For production deployments, use a process manager like **Supervisor** or **systemd** to manage Gunicorn processes. This will ensure that Gunicorn is automatically restarted if it crashes and starts at boot time.

- **Supervisor**: Install Supervisor and configure it to manage Gunicorn.
- **systemd**: Create a service file for Gunicorn and manage it with `systemctl`.

Configuring a Production Database and Setting Up Environments

1. Production Database Setup

In production, you'll likely be using a more robust database like PostgreSQL, MySQL, or MariaDB instead of SQLite (which is commonly used in development). Here's an example configuration for PostgreSQL in your `settings.py`:

```python
# settings.py
```

```
DATABASES = {
    'default': {
        'ENGINE':
'django.db.backends.postgresql',
        'NAME': os.getenv('DB_NAME'),
        'USER': os.getenv('DB_USER'),
        'PASSWORD': os.getenv('DB_PASSWORD'),
        'HOST':             os.getenv('DB_HOST',
'localhost'),
        'PORT': os.getenv('DB_PORT', '5432'),
    }
}
```

Make sure to configure the database and set the corresponding environment variables in your production environment.

2. Database Migrations

Before running your application in production, apply any migrations to ensure your database schema is up to date:

```
bash
```

```
python manage.py migrate
```

3. Configuring Environment Variables for Production

Use environment variables to manage settings such as database credentials, secret keys, and other sensitive data. This keeps your production environment secure.

229

For example, use a `.env` file or set environment variables directly on your server:

```text
```

```text
DJANGO_SECRET_KEY=your_production_secret_key
DB_NAME=your_db_name
DB_USER=your_db_user
DB_PASSWORD=your_db_password
```

Then, load these variables into Django's `settings.py` file using `python-dotenv` or the `os` module, as shown in the previous section.

4. Setting Up Environments

You might want to separate your development, staging, and production environments. You can achieve this by using different `settings.py` files or setting environment-specific variables.

- **Option 1: Multiple Settings Files** Create different settings files for different environments, like `settings_dev.py`, `settings_prod.py`, and switch between them by setting the `DJANGO_SETTINGS_MODULE` environment variable.

```bash
```

```
export
DJANGO_SETTINGS_MODULE=myproject.settings_prod
```

- **Option 2: Environment-Specific Variables**
  Use environment variables to load different settings for each environment. For instance, the `DEBUG` setting could be set as `False` in production and `True` in development using environment variables.

```python
python
```

```python
DEBUG = os.getenv('DJANGO_DEBUG', 'False') ==
'True'
```

Best Practices for Deployment

1. Use a Reverse Proxy (Nginx or Apache)

For better performance and security, it's common to use a reverse proxy like **Nginx** or **Apache** to serve your Django application. These web servers can handle incoming requests, serve static files, and pass dynamic requests to Gunicorn. They also provide security features like SSL termination and rate limiting.

Example of Nginx configuration:

```nginx
nginx
```

```nginx
server {
    listen 80;
```

```
server_name yourdomain.com;

location / {
    proxy_pass http://127.0.0.1:8000;
    proxy_set_header Host $host;
    proxy_set_header X-Real-IP $remote_addr;
    proxy_set_header         X-Forwarded-For
$proxy_add_x_forwarded_for;
    }

location /static/ {
    alias /path/to/your/static/;
    }

location /media/ {
    alias /path/to/your/media/;
    }
}
```

2. Enable SSL/TLS for Secure Connections

Use SSL/TLS (HTTPS) to encrypt communication between the client and the server. You can use **Let's Encrypt** for free SSL certificates, or configure SSL with a service like **AWS Certificate Manager** for production environments.

3. Monitor and Backup Your Application

In production, you should actively monitor your application using tools like **Sentry**, **New Relic**, or **Datadog** for error tracking and performance monitoring. Additionally, set up automatic backups for your database and static files to prevent data loss.

4. Regularly Update Dependencies

Ensure that your application is using up-to-date libraries and dependencies. Regularly run `pip freeze` to check for outdated dependencies, and use a tool like **Dependabot** or **PyUp** to manage updates automatically.

5. Test Your Deployment

Before pushing changes to production, always test your deployment process. Set up staging or testing environments to simulate production conditions and catch any potential issues.

Summary

In this chapter, we covered how to deploy a Django application from a local development environment to a production server. We walked through:

- Preparing your Django project for production, including setting `DEBUG` to `False`, configuring environment variables, and managing static/media files.

- Deploying Django with Gunicorn and WSGI, and setting up a reverse proxy with Nginx.
- Configuring a production database, setting up environments, and using environment-specific settings.

By following these steps and best practices, you can ensure that your Django application is secure, performant, and ready for production.

CHAPTER 22

WORKING WITH DJANGO SECURITY FEATURES

Django provides a robust set of security features that help protect your web application from common vulnerabilities and security threats. From securing user data to preventing attacks such as cross-site scripting (XSS), cross-site request forgery (CSRF), and SQL injection, Django helps ensure your application remains secure by default. In this chapter, we will explore Django's security features, how to secure user data and passwords, and discuss common security practices to avoid vulnerabilities.

Introduction to Django's Security Features

Django takes security seriously and provides several built-in mechanisms to safeguard against common web application vulnerabilities. These mechanisms help developers avoid pitfalls by providing safe defaults, securing user data, and mitigating attack risks.

Some key security features in Django include:

- **Cross-Site Request Forgery (CSRF) Protection**: Prevents unauthorized commands being transmitted from a user who is tricked into submitting a request.

- **Cross-Site Scripting (XSS) Protection**: Prevents attackers from injecting malicious JavaScript into web pages.

- **SQL Injection Protection**: Ensures that queries executed through Django ORM are safe from SQL injection.

- **Clickjacking Protection**: Protects your website from being embedded in an iframe and used in clickjacking attacks.

- **Password Hashing**: Ensures that passwords are stored securely using cryptographic hash functions, so even if your database is compromised, the passwords remain safe.

Securing User Data, Passwords, and Sessions

1. Securing User Passwords

Django uses strong hashing algorithms by default to securely store user passwords. The password is never stored in plain text but is instead hashed using a secure algorithm, making it nearly impossible for attackers to retrieve the original password from the stored hash.

- **Password Hashing in Django**: Django uses **PBKDF2** as the default password hashing algorithm, which is a secure and widely accepted algorithm. You can easily change the hashing algorithm if needed (e.g., to bcrypt or Argon2) via the `PASSWORD_HASHERS` setting.

Example: Password Hashing Settings

```python
# settings.py
PASSWORD_HASHERS = [

'django.contrib.auth.hashers.PBKDF2PasswordHash
er',

'django.contrib.auth.hashers.PBKDF2SHA1Password
Hasher',

'django.contrib.auth.hashers.BCryptSHA256Passwo
rdHasher',

'django.contrib.auth.hashers.Argon2PasswordHash
er',  # Most secure choice
]
```

- **Using `make_password` and `check_password`**: When dealing with passwords programmatically (e.g., during user registration or login), you can use Django's `make_password()` and `check_password()` functions to ensure passwords are securely hashed and checked.

```python
python

from      django.contrib.auth.hashers      import
make_password, check_password

# Hashing a password
hashed_password = make_password('my_password')

# Verifying a password
if              check_password('my_password',
hashed_password):
    print("Password is correct!")
```

2. Securing User Sessions

Django's session framework helps you manage user sessions securely. It stores session data on the server (in a database, cache, or file system) and uses a session ID stored in the user's browser to retrieve the session data.

Session Security Features:

- **Session Cookies**: By default, Django sets the `SESSION_COOKIE_SECURE` flag to `True` in production, ensuring that session cookies are only transmitted over HTTPS, protecting them from interception by attackers.

- **Session Expiry**: Django provides configurable session expiration to prevent session hijacking. You can set a session timeout to automatically log users out after a period of inactivity.

Example: Session Settings

```python
python

# settings.py

# Ensure that session cookies are only sent over
HTTPS (in production)
SESSION_COOKIE_SECURE = True

# Set session timeout to 30 minutes
SESSION_COOKIE_AGE = 1800   # Time in seconds
SESSION_EXPIRE_AT_BROWSER_CLOSE = True   # Expire
session when browser is closed
```

3. Securing User Data

It's essential to store sensitive user data securely. Here are some best practices to follow:

- **Encryption**: Use encryption for sensitive data like personal information, credit card numbers, or health records. Django does not provide built-in encryption for

239

this type of data, but you can integrate third-party libraries like **cryptography** to encrypt sensitive fields.

- **Use   django-encrypted-model-fields   for encrypting model fields**.

```bash
bash
```

```
pip install django-encrypted-model-fields
python
```

```python
from encrypted_fields import EncryptedCharField

class UserProfile(models.Model):
    name = models.CharField(max_length=100)
    social_security_number           =
EncryptedCharField(max_length=20)
```

- **Use EmailField**: When collecting emails, Django provides an EmailField that ensures the value is a valid email format and performs basic validation automatically.

Common Security Practices and Avoiding Vulnerabilities

1. Cross-Site Request Forgery (CSRF) Protection

CSRF attacks occur when an attacker tricks a user into making an unwanted request to a web application where the user is authenticated, such as submitting a form or making a sensitive request.

- **Django's CSRF Protection**: Django includes built-in CSRF protection for forms and AJAX requests. It does this by generating a unique CSRF token for each form submission and checking that the token matches the one submitted by the user.

To include the CSRF token in your templates, use the `{% csrf_token %}` tag inside your form:

html

```
<form method="POST">
    {% csrf_token %}
    <input type="text" name="username">
    <input type="submit" value="Submit">
</form>
```

For AJAX requests, Django's CSRF protection can be enabled using the `X-CSRFToken` header. You can retrieve the CSRF token from the cookie and include it in your AJAX requests.

javascript

```
$.ajax({
    type: 'POST',
    url: '/your-url/',
    headers: {
        'X-CSRFToken': Cookies.get('csrftoken')
// Fetch from the CSRF cookie
```

241

```
    },
    data: { your_data: 'value' }
});
```

2. Cross-Site Scripting (XSS) Protection

XSS attacks occur when an attacker injects malicious JavaScript into a website, which is then executed in a user's browser. Django automatically escapes variables in templates to prevent XSS attacks, meaning that any data inserted into HTML templates will be automatically escaped to prevent harmful code execution.

- **Avoiding XSS**: Never insert unescaped user input directly into JavaScript, HTML, or URLs. Use Django's template syntax, which automatically escapes any data:

```html
```

```
<p>{{   user_input    }}</p>       <!--   Django
automatically escapes user_input -->
```

If you need to insert raw HTML, use the |safe filter cautiously:

```html
```

```
<p>{{ user_input|safe }}</p>   <!-- Be very
careful when using this, as it disables escaping
-->
```

242

3. SQL Injection Protection

SQL injection attacks occur when an attacker is able to manipulate SQL queries to access or modify your database. Django ORM automatically uses parameterized queries, which makes it resistant to SQL injection by default.

Example:

```python
# Safe query
user = User.objects.get(username="username")

# Unsafe query (vulnerable to SQL injection)
user = User.objects.raw("SELECT * FROM app_user
WHERE username='%s'" % user_input)
```

With Django ORM, always use the provided query methods (`filter`, `get`, etc.) to avoid direct SQL queries, as they ensure the use of parameterized queries.

4. Clickjacking Protection

Clickjacking attacks occur when a website is embedded in an invisible iframe and the user is tricked into clicking on something without realizing it. Django's **Clickjacking protection** prevents this by adding the `X-Frame-Options` header to responses, which prevents your site from being embedded in an iframe.

Example: Enabling Clickjacking Protection

python

```
# settings.py
X_FRAME_OPTIONS = 'DENY'  # Prevent any domain
from embedding your site in an iframe
```

You can also use `X_FRAME_OPTIONS = 'SAMEORIGIN'` to allow your site to be embedded in an iframe on the same domain.

5. Secure Session Management

Ensure that sessions are managed securely by:

- Setting `SESSION_COOKIE_SECURE` to `True` to ensure cookies are only transmitted over HTTPS.
- Using a **strong session ID** by setting `SESSION_ENGINE = 'django.contrib.sessions.backends.cache'` or other secure backends.

6. Content Security Policy (CSP)

Implementing a **Content Security Policy (CSP)** helps prevent a range of attacks, including XSS and data injection attacks, by specifying which resources can be loaded on your website. You can add CSP headers to your app using third-party libraries like **django-csp**.

```bash
pip install django-csp
```

Then, configure the CSP in your settings:

```python
# settings.py
INSTALLED_APPS = [
    'csp',
]


CSP_DEFAULT_SRC = ("'self'",)
CSP_SCRIPT_SRC             =             ("'self'",
'https://apis.google.com')
```

Summary

In this chapter, we discussed **Django's built-in security features** and how to protect your application from common web vulnerabilities. We covered securing user data and passwords, preventing CSRF and XSS attacks, protecting against SQL injection, and implementing clickjacking protection.

By following these security practices and using Django's built-in tools, you can create a robust, secure web application that protects user data and guards against a variety of potential attacks. Always stay vigilant about security and ensure your Django application remains up to date with the latest security patches and best practices.

CHAPTER 23

DJANGO PERFORMANCE OPTIMIZATION

Performance optimization is a crucial part of building and maintaining a Django application, especially as it scales. Optimizing your Django app can result in faster response times, reduced server load, and better user experience. In this chapter, we will cover key strategies for improving performance in Django, including database indexing, query optimization, caching strategies, and load balancing for scaling your Django app.

Database Indexing and Query Optimization

1. Understanding Database Indexing

A **database index** is a data structure that helps speed up retrieval operations on a database table at the cost of additional space and slower write operations (insertions, updates, deletions). Indexes are crucial for improving the speed of queries that involve filtering, sorting, and joining large datasets.

- **Why   Use   Indexes?**
  Indexing speeds up query performance, especially when dealing with large tables or complex queries. By default,

Django creates indexes on primary keys and foreign keys, but you may need to create additional indexes for columns that are frequently queried.

- **Types of Indexes**:
  - ○ **Single-Column Index**: Indexes a single column in the database.
  - ○ **Multi-Column Index**: Indexes multiple columns to improve performance for queries that filter by more than one column.
  - ○ **Unique Index**: Ensures that the values in a column are unique.
  - ○ **Partial Index**: Indexes a subset of rows, based on a condition.

2. Creating Indexes in Django Models

In Django, you can define indexes using the `Meta` class within a model. Django also provides options to define composite indexes on multiple fields.

```python
python

from django.db import models

class Post(models.Model):
    title = models.CharField(max_length=100)
    content = models.TextField()
    published_date = models.DateTimeField()
```

```
class Meta:
    indexes = [
        models.Index(fields=['title']),    #
Single-column index

models.Index(fields=['published_date',
'title']),   # Composite index
    ]
```

In the example above:

- An index is created on the `title` field to speed up lookups using `title`.
- A composite index is created on both `published_date` and `title` to optimize queries that filter by both columns.

3. Optimizing Queries

Inefficient database queries can slow down your Django app. Here are a few techniques to optimize database queries:

- **Avoid N+1 Query Problem**: Django's ORM is susceptible to the N+1 query problem, where it makes a separate query for each related object, leading to excessive database calls.

    Fix: Use `select_related()` for `ForeignKey` and `OneToOneField` relationships, and

```
prefetch_related()    for    ManyToManyField
```
relationships.

```
python
```

```
# Example: Using select_related to optimize
queries
posts                                        =
Post.objects.select_related('author').all
()
```

- o **select_related**: This is used for **forward** relationships (e.g., `ForeignKey`), and it performs a SQL join to fetch the related objects in a single query.
- o **prefetch_related**: This is used for **many-to-many** relationships or reverse relationships and performs separate queries but combines them in Python.

- **Use `only()` and `defer()` for Query Optimization**: When retrieving model instances, you may only need a subset of fields. Using `only()` and `defer()` can limit the fields that are loaded, reducing memory usage.

```
python
```

```
# Fetch only selected fields
```

```
posts       =        Post.objects.only('title',
'published_date')
```

- o **only()**: Fetches only the specified fields.

- o **defer()**: Loads all fields except those specified.

- **Using values() and values_list()**: When you don't need complete model instances, use `values()` and `values_list()` to fetch only the required fields as dictionaries or tuples, which is more efficient than fetching full model objects.

python

```
# Fetch only 'title' and 'published_date'
posts       =        Post.objects.values('title',
'published_date')
```

4. Database Query Profiling

You can profile your queries to identify slow queries. Django provides a `connection.queries` attribute that stores all SQL queries executed during the request.

python

```
from django.db import connection

# Execute some queries
posts = Post.objects.all()
```

251

```
# Print the queries
print(connection.queries)
```

By analyzing these queries, you can identify inefficient queries and optimize them accordingly.

Caching Strategies for Faster Responses

Caching is one of the most effective ways to improve the performance of your Django application by storing the result of expensive queries or computations and reusing them instead of recomputing them each time.

1. Using Django's Cache Framework

Django's cache framework supports multiple cache backends, including in-memory caching, file-based caching, and third-party caching solutions like Memcached and Redis.

- **Basic Caching Example (in-memory):**

```python
from django.core.cache import cache

# Set a cache value
cache.set('some_key',                'some_value',
timeout=60*15)  # 15 minutes timeout
```

```
# Retrieve a cache value
value = cache.get('some_key')
```

2. Caching Views with cache_page

Django allows you to cache the output of entire views for a set amount of time. This is particularly useful for pages with static content that doesn't change frequently.

python

```
from    django.views.decorators.cache    import
cache_page

@cache_page(60 * 15)   # Cache for 15 minutes
def my_view(request):
    # Expensive logic here
    return render(request, 'my_template.html')
```

3. Template Fragment Caching

For parts of your template that change infrequently but are expensive to render, you can cache fragments of your templates.

html

```
{% load cache %}
{% cache 600 sidebar %}
    <!-- Expensive sidebar logic here -->
```

253

```
{% endcache %}
```

In this example, the sidebar is cached for 600 seconds (10 minutes), reducing the rendering cost for each request.

4. Using Redis or Memcached for Advanced Caching

For high-traffic applications, it's often more efficient to use an external cache store like **Redis** or **Memcached** instead of the default in-memory cache.

- **Redis Configuration in Django**:

```bash
pip install django-redis
python
```

```python
# settings.py
CACHES = {
    'default': {
        'BACKEND':
'django_redis.cache.RedisCache',
        'LOCATION':
'redis://127.0.0.1:6379/1',        #    Redis
server location
        'OPTIONS': {
            'CLIENT_CLASS':
'django_redis.client.DefaultClient',
        }
```

```
        }

    }
```

5. Database Query Caching

You can cache the results of expensive database queries. For example, if you're executing the same query repeatedly, you can cache the result and fetch it from the cache for subsequent requests.

```python
python

# Cache the query result
posts = cache.get('posts_cache')
if not posts:
    posts = Post.objects.all()
    cache.set('posts_cache',            posts,
timeout=60*15)
```

Load Balancing and Scaling Your Django App

As your application grows, you may need to scale it to handle more traffic and reduce the load on individual servers. Here are some techniques for scaling and load balancing your Django application.

1. Load Balancing

Load balancing involves distributing incoming traffic across multiple servers to ensure that no single server is overwhelmed with too many requests. This can improve the reliability and performance of your Django app.

- **Using Nginx for Load Balancing**: You can configure **Nginx** as a reverse proxy and load balancer for your Django application. Nginx can forward requests to multiple Gunicorn instances running on different servers or on different ports of the same server.

Example Nginx load balancing configuration:

```nginx
upstream django {
    server 127.0.0.1:8001;
    server 127.0.0.1:8002;
}

server {
    listen 80;
    server_name yourdomain.com;

    location / {
        proxy_pass http://django;
        proxy_set_header Host $host;
        proxy_set_header X-Real-IP $remote_addr;
        proxy_set_header         X-Forwarded-For
$proxy_add_x_forwarded_for;
    }
```

}

2. Horizontal Scaling

Horizontal scaling means adding more servers to distribute the load. You can use cloud platforms like **AWS**, **Google Cloud**, or **Heroku** to automatically scale your Django application horizontally.

- **Using AWS Elastic Beanstalk**: AWS Elastic Beanstalk can automatically handle scaling by adding more instances based on traffic. It simplifies deployment, monitoring, and scaling.

3. Vertical Scaling

Vertical scaling refers to adding more resources (CPU, RAM) to an individual server. While this can be effective for smaller-scale applications, it has limitations in comparison to horizontal scaling, which distributes the load across multiple servers.

4. Database Scaling

As your app grows, the database can become a bottleneck. Here are some strategies for scaling the database:

- **Database Sharding**: Split your database across multiple servers to distribute the load. Each shard can hold a subset of data.

257

- **Read/Write Splitting**: Use a master-slave database setup where the master database handles write operations, and the slave databases handle read operations.
- **Database Caching**: Cache frequently accessed data to reduce the number of database queries.

5. Asynchronous Task Processing

For long-running tasks, such as sending emails or processing large files, consider using an asynchronous task queue with a tool like **Celery**. This allows your app to process tasks in the background, improving performance by freeing up resources for other requests.

Example: Using Celery

bash

```
pip install celery
```

Set up a Celery task to handle background jobs:

python

```
from celery import shared_task

@shared_task
def send_email_task():
    # Your email sending logic here
    pass
```

258

Then, run Celery worker processes alongside your Django app to process background tasks.

Summary

In this chapter, we covered key strategies for **optimizing Django application performance**. We discussed:

- **Database indexing and query optimization**: Using indexes and optimizing queries to improve database performance.
- **Caching strategies**: Implementing caching for faster response times, including view, template, and database query caching.
- **Load balancing and scaling**: Distributing traffic across multiple servers and using horizontal and vertical scaling techniques to ensure your app can handle increasing traffic.

By applying these performance optimization techniques, you can improve the efficiency of your Django application, ensuring a smoother experience for users as your app grows.

CHAPTER 24

BUILDING A FULL-FLEDGED WEB APPLICATION WITH DJANGO

Building a full-fledged web application with Django involves several stages, from planning the app and defining the requirements to deploying it and managing the database. In this chapter, we will walk through the process of building a complete web application using Django, focusing on:

1. Planning the app and setting up your project.
2. Creating models, views, templates, and forms.
3. Working with third-party libraries and APIs.
4. Deploying the app to a production environment.

Step-by-Step Guide to Building a Complete Web App

Let's walk through the essential steps involved in building a web application from start to finish.

1. Planning the Application

Before diving into coding, it's essential to plan the application. The key steps include:

- **Defining the app's purpose**: What is the app supposed to do? Who are the users?
- **Identifying features**: Break down the features you want to implement, such as user registration, data storage, authentication, etc.
- **Sketching the UI**: Consider how the user interface will look, including the layout, navigation, and key components.
- **Modeling the data**: Identify the models you will need to store data (e.g., Users, Posts, Comments).

Example: Building a Blog App

Let's say we're building a simple **blog application**. The app will allow users to:

- Register and log in.
- Create, edit, and delete blog posts.
- Leave comments on posts.

We'll need the following models:

- **User**: This will be handled by Django's built-in `User` model.
- **Post**: This model will store blog posts.
- **Comment**: This model will store comments for each blog post.

2. Setting Up Your Django Project

Start by creating a new Django project and app.

```bash
bash

# Create a new Django project
django-admin startproject myblog

# Navigate to the project directory
cd myblog

# Create a new app within the project
python manage.py startapp blog
```

3. Creating Models

Define models for your app by editing the `models.py` file inside your app.

```python
python

# blog/models.py
from django.db import models
from django.contrib.auth.models import User

class Post(models.Model):
    title = models.CharField(max_length=200)
    content = models.TextField()
```

262

```
    author          =           models.ForeignKey(User,
on_delete=models.CASCADE)
    created_at                                    =
models.DateTimeField(auto_now_add=True)
    updated_at                                    =
models.DateTimeField(auto_now=True)

    def __str__(self):
        return self.title

class Comment(models.Model):
    post            =           models.ForeignKey(Post,
on_delete=models.CASCADE,
related_name='comments')
    author = models.CharField(max_length=100)
    content = models.TextField()
    created_at                                    =
models.DateTimeField(auto_now_add=True)

    def __str__(self):
        return f"Comment by {self.author} on
{self.post.title}"
```

Here, we have two models:

- Post: Represents a blog post with a title, content, author
  (a ForeignKey to the User model), and timestamps for
  when the post was created and last updated.

263

- Comment: Represents a comment on a post with the content and author.

Run the migration to create the tables for these models in the database:

```bash
```

```
python manage.py makemigrations
python manage.py migrate
```

4. Creating Views and URLs

Next, create views to handle requests and render templates. We'll define views for listing posts, viewing a single post, and creating comments.

In views.py:

```python
```

```python
# blog/views.py
from    django.shortcuts    import    render,
get_object_or_404
from .models import Post, Comment
from django.http import HttpResponseRedirect
from django.urls import reverse

def post_list(request):
```

```
    posts     =      Post.objects.all().order_by('-
created_at')
    return                    render(request,
'blog/post_list.html', {'posts': posts})

def post_detail(request, pk):
    post = get_object_or_404(Post, pk=pk)
    comments = post.comments.all()
    if request.method == 'POST':
        comment_content                         =
request.POST.get('content')
        Comment.objects.create(post=post,
author=request.user.username,
content=comment_content)
        return
HttpResponseRedirect(reverse('post_detail',
args=[pk]))
    return                    render(request,
'blog/post_detail.html',      {'post':      post,
'comments': comments})
```

- `post_list` renders a list of all blog posts.
- `post_detail` displays a single post with the option to add comments.

In `urls.py`, define URLs to link the views:

```
python
```

```
# blog/urls.py
from django.urls import path
from . import views

urlpatterns = [
    path('', views.post_list, name='post_list'),
    path('post/<int:pk>/',    views.post_detail,
name='post_detail'),
]
```

Now, include these URLs in the main project's `urls.py`:

```
python
```

```
# myblog/urls.py
from django.contrib import admin
from django.urls import path, include

urlpatterns = [
    path('admin/', admin.site.urls),
    path('',  include('blog.urls')),    # Include
the blog app's URLs
]
```

5. Creating Templates

Next, create templates to render the views. In the `blog/templates/blog/` directory, create `post_list.html` and `post_detail.html`.

266

post_list.html:

html

```
<!-- blog/templates/blog/post_list.html -->
<h1>Blog Posts</h1>
{% for post in posts %}
    <h2><a href="{% url 'post_detail' post.pk
%}">{{ post.title }}</a></h2>
    <p>{{ post.content|truncatewords:20 }}</p>
{% endfor %}
```

post_detail.html:

html

```
<!-- blog/templates/blog/post_detail.html -->
<h1>{{ post.title }}</h1>
<p>{{ post.content }}</p>
<h3>Comments:</h3>
{% for comment in comments %}
    <p><strong>{{ comment.author }}:</strong> {{
comment.content }}</p>
{% endfor %}
<form method="POST">
    {% csrf_token %}
    <textarea name="content" placeholder="Write
a comment"></textarea>
    <button type="submit">Post Comment</button>
</form>
```

267

6. Working with Forms

To allow users to submit blog posts or comments, we use Django's `forms` module.

Creating a form for creating posts:

python

```python
# blog/forms.py
from django import forms
from .models import Post

class PostForm(forms.ModelForm):
    class Meta:
        model = Post
        fields = ['title', 'content']
```

Use the form in a view for creating posts:

python

```python
# blog/views.py
from .forms import PostForm

def create_post(request):
    if request.method == 'POST':
        form = PostForm(request.POST)
        if form.is_valid():
            form.save()
```

```
        return HttpResponseRedirect('/')
    else:
        form = PostForm()
    return                          render(request,
'blog/create_post.html', {'form': form})
```

Add the URL for this view:

```python
python
```

```
# blog/urls.py
urlpatterns = [
    path('', views.post_list, name='post_list'),
    path('post/<int:pk>/',     views.post_detail,
name='post_detail'),
    path('create/',            views.create_post,
name='create_post'),
]
```

7. Working with Third-Party Libraries and APIs

Django's flexibility allows you to integrate with third-party libraries and APIs. For example, if you want to integrate a social media share button or use an external API, you can use libraries like **Requests** to interact with external services.

Example: Using the Requests library:

```bash
bash
```

```
pip install requests
python

import requests

def fetch_external_data(request):
    response                                =
requests.get('https://api.example.com/data')
    data = response.json()
    return                     render(request,
'blog/external_data.html', {'data': data})
```

8. Deploying the Application

Once the application is developed, it's time to deploy it to production. Here's a quick overview of deploying a Django app:

- **Prepare for Production**: Set `DEBUG = False`, configure `ALLOWED_HOSTS`, set up static files with `collectstatic`, and configure a production database.
- **Use Gunicorn for WSGI**: Install **Gunicorn** and configure it to run the application.

```bash
pip install gunicorn
gunicorn myblog.wsgi:application
```

- **Configure Nginx**: Set up Nginx as a reverse proxy to handle traffic and serve static files.
- **Use a Database**: In production, you should use a database like PostgreSQL or MySQL instead of SQLite.
- **Set up HTTPS**: Use a service like **Let's Encrypt** to configure SSL for secure HTTPS connections.

9. Best Practices

- **Version Control**: Use Git for version control, commit frequently, and push your code to repositories like GitHub or GitLab.
- **Testing**: Write tests to ensure your app works as expected. Use Django's test framework to write unit tests for views, models, and forms.
- **Monitoring and Logging**: Set up monitoring tools (e.g., **Sentry**, **New Relic**) and logging to track errors and performance in production.
- **Security**: Follow Django's security best practices, such as using strong password hashing, CSRF protection, and enabling HTTPS.

Summary

In this chapter, we walked through the process of building a full-fledged web application with Django. We covered the entire process, from planning the application and setting up models to deploying the app and working with third-party libraries. By following these steps and practices, you can build robust, scalable, and secure Django web applications.

CHAPTER 25

INTRODUCTION TO DJANGO CHANNELS FOR REAL-TIME WEB APPS

Real-time web applications, such as chat apps, live notifications, and live data updates, provide a more interactive experience for users by enabling instant communication between the client and the server. Django Channels extends Django to handle asynchronous protocols like WebSockets, allowing you to build these real-time features in your Django app.

In this chapter, we will cover:

- What Django Channels are and how they work.
- How to build real-time features with WebSockets using Django Channels.
- How to use Django Channels to implement chat, notifications, and live updates in your web app.

What are Django Channels?

Django Channels is an extension to Django that enables Django to handle asynchronous communication, such as WebSockets,

HTTP/2, and background tasks. It allows Django to support long-lived network connections, making it ideal for real-time features.

Django traditionally operates in a synchronous request-response cycle, where the server handles one request at a time. This is fine for standard HTTP-based applications but becomes inefficient for applications that need to maintain a persistent connection with the client, like chat apps or live notifications.

Key Features of Django Channels:

- **WebSocket Support**: Allows the server to maintain a persistent connection with the client for bidirectional communication, enabling real-time features.
- **Asynchronous Task Handling**: Helps with background tasks, such as processing long-running requests without blocking the main thread.
- **Support for Protocols like HTTP/2**: Channels can handle other communication protocols like HTTP/2, which is beneficial for more efficient real-time interactions.

Building Real-Time Features with WebSockets

A **WebSocket** is a protocol that provides full-duplex communication channels over a single TCP connection, which allows for bidirectional communication between the server and client. WebSockets are ideal for applications that need low-latency updates or push notifications, such as chat rooms, live feeds, and multiplayer games.

With Django Channels, you can easily integrate WebSockets into your Django project.

1. Installing Django Channels

To get started with Django Channels, you need to install the channels package.

bash

```
pip install channels
```

Next, add channels to your INSTALLED_APPS in settings.py:

python

```
# settings.py
INSTALLED_APPS = [
    # Other apps...
    'channels',
]
```

Then, configure Channels as the default application for handling requests by setting ASGI_APPLICATION in settings.py:

python

```python
# settings.py
ASGI_APPLICATION = "myproject.asgi.application"
```

Create an `asgi.py` file in your project directory (where `settings.py` is located). This file defines the application that will handle your ASGI (Asynchronous Server Gateway Interface) connections.

python

```python
# myproject/asgi.py
import os
from channels.routing import ProtocolTypeRouter, URLRouter
from channels.auth import AuthMiddlewareStack
from django.urls import path
from blog import consumers  # Assuming we create WebSocket consumers in the 'blog' app

os.environ.setdefault('DJANGO_SETTINGS_MODULE', 'myproject.settings')

application = ProtocolTypeRouter({
    "http": get_asgi_application(),
    "websocket": AuthMiddlewareStack(
        URLRouter([
```

```
        path('ws/chat/',
consumers.ChatConsumer.as_asgi()),    # URL path
for WebSocket
        ])
    ),
})
```

Here:

- `ProtocolTypeRouter` is used to route the requests based on the protocol type (HTTP or WebSocket).
- `AuthMiddlewareStack` handles user authentication for WebSocket connections.

2. Creating a WebSocket Consumer

Consumers in Django Channels are similar to views in Django but handle WebSocket connections instead of HTTP requests. A WebSocket consumer is responsible for handling messages sent from the client, as well as sending messages back to the client.

Let's create a simple chat consumer.

```
python
```

```python
# blog/consumers.py
import json
from      channels.generic.websocket      import
AsyncWebsocketConsumer
```

277

```python
class ChatConsumer(AsyncWebsocketConsumer):
    async def connect(self):
        # This is the method that is called when
a WebSocket connection is established.
        self.room_name = 'chat_room'
        self.room_group_name                    =
f'chat_{self.room_name}'

        # Join the room group
        await self.channel_layer.group_add(
            self.room_group_name,
            self.channel_name
        )

        # Accept the WebSocket connection
        await self.accept()

    async def disconnect(self, close_code):
        # This is the method that is called when
the WebSocket connection is closed.
        await self.channel_layer.group_discard(
            self.room_group_name,
            self.channel_name
        )

    async def receive(self, text_data):
        # This method handles incoming WebSocket
messages
```

```
    text_data_json = json.loads(text_data)
    message = text_data_json['message']

    # Send message to the room group
    await self.channel_layer.group_send(
        self.room_group_name,
        {
            'type': 'chat_message',
            'message': message
        }
    )

async def chat_message(self, event):
    # This method sends a message to the
WebSocket
    message = event['message']
    await self.send(text_data=json.dumps({
        'message': message
    }))
```

In the ChatConsumer class:

- connect: This method is called when a WebSocket connection is established. It joins the user to a group, which allows broadcasting messages to all connected users.
- disconnect: This method is called when the WebSocket connection is closed. It removes the user from the group.

- receive: This method processes the message received from the WebSocket. It extracts the message and sends it to all users in the same chat room.
- chat_message: This method sends a message to the WebSocket when a message is broadcasted in the group.

3. Setting up Channels Layer (Redis)

Django Channels uses a **channel layer** to facilitate communication between consumers. The channel layer can be backed by Redis, a fast in-memory data store. Install Redis and the channels_redis package:

bash

```
pip install channels_redis
```

Then, configure Redis as the channel layer backend in settings.py:

python

```
# settings.py
CHANNEL_LAYERS = {
    'default': {
        'BACKEND':
'channels_redis.core.RedisChannelLayer',
        'CONFIG': {
```

```
        "hosts": [('127.0.0.1', 6379)],    #
Redis server configuration
        },
    },
}
```

Make sure that Redis is installed and running on your machine, or use a Redis service like **RedisLabs** for a managed Redis instance.

Using Channels for Chat, Notifications, and Live Updates

1. Real-Time Chat Application

We already set up the WebSocket connection in the `ChatConsumer` for a basic chat application. Let's implement the front end for the WebSocket connection.

In `chat.html`:

html

```
<!-- chat.html -->
<script>
    const chatSocket = new WebSocket(
        'ws://'   +   window.location.host   +
'/ws/chat/'
    );

    chatSocket.onmessage = function(e) {
```

```
        const data = JSON.parse(e.data);
        document.querySelector('#chat-
log').value += (data.message + '\n');
    };


    chatSocket.onclose = function(e) {
        console.error('Chat     socket     closed
unexpectedly');
    };


    document.querySelector('#chat-message-
input').focus();
    document.querySelector('#chat-message-
input').onkeyup = function(e) {
        if (e.keyCode === 13) {  // Enter key
            const       messageInputDom       =
document.querySelector('#chat-message-input');
            const         message         =
messageInputDom.value;
            chatSocket.send(JSON.stringify({
                'message': message
            }));
            messageInputDom.value = '';
        }
    };
</script>
```

In this HTML:

- The WebSocket connection is established when the page loads.
- When a message is received, it is appended to the chat log.
- The user can send messages by typing and pressing Enter.

2. Real-Time Notifications

You can use Channels to implement real-time notifications. For example, when a new comment is added to a blog post, all users can be notified in real-time.

Modify the consumer to handle different types of events, such as notifications.

python

```python
# blog/consumers.py

class
NotificationConsumer(AsyncWebsocketConsumer):
    async def connect(self):
        self.user_group_name              =
f'user_{self.scope["user"].id}'

        await self.channel_layer.group_add(
            self.user_group_name,
            self.channel_name
        )
```

283

```
        await self.accept()

    async def disconnect(self, close_code):
        await self.channel_layer.group_discard(
            self.user_group_name,
            self.channel_name
        )

    async def send_notification(self, event):
        notification = event['notification']
        await self.send(text_data=json.dumps({
            'notification': notification
        }))
```

In this example, each user has a unique notification group. When an event occurs (e.g., a comment is added), you can send a notification to that user in real-time.

3. Real-Time Live Updates

You can also use Django Channels to implement live updates, such as displaying live stock prices or user activity. This can be done similarly to the chat application, where data is broadcasted to the client via WebSockets.

Summary

In this chapter, we explored how to build real-time web applications using **Django Channels**. We covered:

- **Django Channels**: An extension to Django that allows for handling WebSockets and asynchronous communication.

- **WebSockets**: A protocol that enables persistent, bidirectional communication between the client and server.

- **Chat, notifications, and live updates**: Examples of how to use Channels to create real-time features like chat applications, live notifications, and live updates.

By integrating Django Channels into your project, you can unlock powerful real-time capabilities, enabling you to build more dynamic and interactive web applications.

CHAPTER 26

ADVANCED DJANGO FEATURES

Django is a powerful web framework that comes with a rich set of features to help developers build robust and scalable applications. In this chapter, we will dive into some of the more advanced features of Django, including **signals and hooks**, using **Celery** for background tasks, and **customizing Django's admin interface**. These features allow for more complex workflows, improve performance, and help tailor the Django experience to suit specific application needs.

Django Signals and Hooks

Django signals are a mechanism that allows different parts of a Django application to communicate and react to specific events or actions. For instance, when a new object is saved to the database, you can use signals to perform additional actions automatically, such as sending an email or updating related objects.

1. What are Django Signals?

Django signals are based on the observer pattern, where one part of the application (the sender) emits a signal, and another part (the receiver) listens for it and reacts when it occurs.

Django provides several built-in signals, such as:

- **pre_save** and **post_save**: Triggered before and after an object is saved to the database.
- **pre_delete** and **post_delete**: Triggered before and after an object is deleted from the database.
- **m2m_changed**: Triggered when a many-to-many relationship changes.

2. Using Django Signals

To use signals, you define a signal receiver function and connect it to a specific signal.

- **Example**: Using post_save signal to send an email after a Post object is created.

python

```python
# blog/signals.py
from django.db.models.signals import post_save
from django.dispatch import receiver
from django.core.mail import send_mail
from .models import Post

@receiver(post_save, sender=Post)
def send_post_creation_email(sender, instance, created, **kwargs):
    if created:
```

```
    send_mail(
        'New Post Created',
        f'A      new      post      titled
"{instance.title}" has been created.',
        'from@example.com',
        ['to@example.com'],
        fail_silently=False,
    )
```

Here, `send_post_creation_email` is connected to the `post_save` signal of the `Post` model. Every time a `Post` is created, this function will be called, sending an email notification.

- **Connecting the Signal**: Ensure the signal is connected when the app is loaded. You can do this in the `apps.py` file of your app.

python

```python
# blog/apps.py
from django.apps import AppConfig

class BlogConfig(AppConfig):
    name = 'blog'

    def ready(self):
        import blog.signals  # Import signals to connect them
```

3. Custom Signals

You can create custom signals for specific events in your application.

python

```
from django.db.models.signals import Signal

# Create a custom signal
custom_signal = Signal()

# Signal receiver function
def custom_signal_handler(sender, **kwargs):
    print("Custom signal received")

# Connecting the signal
custom_signal.connect(custom_signal_handler)

# Sending the signal
custom_signal.send(sender=None)
```

In this example:

- A custom signal `custom_signal` is created and connected to a handler.
- The signal is sent with `custom_signal.send(sender=None)`.

289

Using Celery for Background Tasks

Celery is a powerful, asynchronous task queue/job queue system that can be used for handling background tasks in Django. It allows you to offload time-consuming operations such as sending emails, processing files, or making API calls to a separate worker process.

1. Setting Up Celery with Django

To use Celery with Django, follow these steps:

- **Install Celery and a message broker (Redis)**:

```bash
pip install celery redis
```

- **Configure Celery in Django**: Create a `celery.py` file in your Django project directory (the same level as `settings.py`):

```python
# myproject/celery.py
from __future__ import absolute_import, unicode_literals
import os
from celery import Celery
```

```
# Set the default Django settings module
for the 'celery' program.
os.environ.setdefault('DJANGO_SETTINGS_MO
DULE', 'myproject.settings')

app = Celery('myproject')

# Using a string here means the worker
doesn't have to serialize
# the configuration object to child
processes.
app.config_from_object('django.conf:setti
ngs', namespace='CELERY')

# Load task modules from all registered
Django app configs.
app.autodiscover_tasks()
```

- **Configure the Celery broker** (Redis) in your
  settings.py:

```
python
```

```
# settings.py
CELERY_BROKER_URL                        =
'redis://localhost:6379/0'
```

- **Create tasks**: In your Django app (e.g., `blog`), create a `tasks.py` file to define the background tasks.

python

```python
# blog/tasks.py
from celery import shared_task

@shared_task
def send_post_creation_email(post_id):
    from .models import Post
    post = Post.objects.get(id=post_id)
    send_mail(
        'New Post Created',
        f'A new post titled "{post.title}" has been created.',
        'from@example.com',
        ['to@example.com'],
        fail_silently=False,
    )
```

- **Calling Celery Tasks**: In your `views.py` or model signal handlers, you can now call Celery tasks asynchronously.

python

```python
# blog/views.py
```

```python
from                .tasks              import
send_post_creation_email

def create_post(request):
    # Create post logic
    post = Post.objects.create(title="New
Post", content="Content")

    send_post_creation_email.delay(post.id)  #
Run this task in the background
```

In this example, when a post is created, the task to send an email is processed asynchronously by Celery.

- **Running Celery**: To process background tasks, start the Celery worker process:

```bash
bash
```

```bash
celery -A myproject worker --loglevel=info
```

- **Running Redis**: Make sure Redis is running on your local machine or use a hosted Redis service.

```bash
bash
```

```bash
redis-server
```

293

Celery is now handling the background tasks asynchronously, which can drastically improve your app's performance by offloading long-running operations to separate worker processes.

Customizing Django's Admin and Other Advanced Features

1. Customizing Django Admin

Django's admin is highly customizable and allows you to tailor the admin interface to your needs.

- **Customizing List Displays**: You can control which fields are shown in the list view in the admin interface.

```python
# blog/admin.py
from django.contrib import admin
from .models import Post

class PostAdmin(admin.ModelAdmin):
    list_display = ('title', 'author',
'created_at', 'updated_at')
    list_filter = ('author', 'created_at')
    search_fields = ('title', 'content')

admin.site.register(Post, PostAdmin)
```

Here:

- o `list_display`: Specifies which fields to display in the list view.
- o `list_filter`: Adds filters in the admin sidebar.
- o `search_fields`: Adds a search box to search for posts by title or content.

- **Customizing Form Fields**: You can customize the form used in the admin interface for a specific model.

python

```python
# blog/admin.py
from django import forms
from .models import Post

class PostForm(forms.ModelForm):
    class Meta:
        model = Post
        fields = ['title', 'content']

    def clean_title(self):
        title = self.cleaned_data['title']
        if "banned" in title:
            raise
forms.ValidationError("Title   contains   a
banned word.")
        return title

class PostAdmin(admin.ModelAdmin):
    form = PostForm
```

295

```
admin.site.register(Post, PostAdmin)
```

- **Inline Models**: You can also embed models as inline forms in the admin interface. This is useful for related models like comments or tags.

python

```python
# blog/admin.py
from django.contrib import admin
from .models import Post, Comment

class CommentInline(admin.TabularInline):
    model = Comment
    extra = 1

class PostAdmin(admin.ModelAdmin):
    inlines = [CommentInline]

admin.site.register(Post, PostAdmin)
```

2. Adding Actions to Admin

Django allows you to add custom actions to the admin interface that apply to selected objects.

python

```python
# blog/admin.py
```

```
from django.contrib import admin
from .models import Post

def mark_posts_as_published(modeladmin, request,
queryset):
    queryset.update(status='published')

class PostAdmin(admin.ModelAdmin):
    actions = [mark_posts_as_published]

admin.site.register(Post, PostAdmin)
```

In this example, the custom action `mark_posts_as_published`
can be selected from the admin interface to mark multiple posts as
published at once.

3. Advanced Model Relationships and Querysets

Django supports advanced relationships between models, such as
many-to-many and many-to-one relationships, and provides
powerful query features to handle complex queries efficiently.
Django's **annotate()** and **aggregate()** functions allow for efficient
database queries and calculations on model data.

```
python
```

```
# Annotate with the number of comments on each
post
from django.db.models import Count
```

```
posts                                              =
Post.objects.annotate(num_comments=Count('comme
nts'))
```

This query annotates each `Post` object with the number of related `Comment` objects, allowing you to access `num_comments` on each post.

Summary

In this chapter, we covered advanced Django features to help you build more complex and performant applications:

- **Django signals and hooks**: We explored how to use Django signals to react to events in your application, such as sending emails when a new post is created.
- **Celery for background tasks**: We learned how to set up Celery to handle long-running tasks asynchronously, improving the performance of your app.
- **Customizing the Django admin**: We explored how to customize the Django admin interface to better suit your needs, including adding custom actions, form validation, and inline models.

These advanced features can significantly enhance your Django projects, improving performance, flexibility, and user experience.

CHAPTER 27

SCALING AND MAINTAINING DJANGO APPLICATIONS

As your Django application grows, it's essential to focus on scaling and maintaining the application to ensure it performs well under increasing load and remains easy to maintain and update. Scaling involves improving performance and handling more users or traffic, while maintaining the codebase involves updating features, fixing bugs, and ensuring the app stays secure and performant.

In this chapter, we will explore:

- Best practices for scaling Django applications.
- Strategies for maintaining and updating the codebase.
- Handling versioning, database management, and deployment.

Best Practices for Scaling Django Apps

Scaling a Django application involves optimizing the infrastructure, databases, and application code to handle more traffic, users, and data. Here are the best practices for scaling Django applications effectively:

1. Horizontal Scaling (Scaling Across Multiple Servers)

Horizontal scaling, also known as **scaling out**, involves adding more machines or instances to your infrastructure to distribute the load. This ensures your application can handle increased traffic by distributing requests across multiple servers.

- **Load Balancing**: Use a load balancer, such as **Nginx**, **HAProxy**, or cloud-based load balancing solutions like **AWS Elastic Load Balancer (ELB)**, to distribute incoming traffic to multiple application servers. This ensures no single server is overwhelmed with too much traffic.

- **Database Replication and Clustering**: For read-heavy applications, implement **read replicas** of your primary database (e.g., PostgreSQL or MySQL). The primary database handles write operations, while the read replicas handle read queries, improving performance.

- **Caching**: Implement caching strategies to reduce database load. Cache frequently accessed data, such as product listings, user profiles, or search results. Use a caching backend like **Redis** or **Memcached** for faster retrieval.

2. Vertical Scaling (Scaling by Upgrading Resources)

Vertical scaling, also known as **scaling up**, involves increasing the resources (CPU, RAM, disk space) of your existing servers. While this can help handle some increases in traffic, it has limitations compared to horizontal scaling, especially for highly scalable applications.

- **Monitor Resources**: Use monitoring tools to track resource usage and identify bottlenecks in your infrastructure. Tools like **Prometheus**, **Grafana**, or **New Relic** can help you identify performance issues in real time.

3. Database Optimization

- **Indexing**: Use database indexing to speed up frequent queries, especially those involving filtering and sorting.
  - Example: Add indexes on frequently queried fields.

```python
class Post(models.Model):
    title                          =
models.CharField(max_length=100)
    created_at = models.DateTimeField()

    class Meta:
        indexes = [
```

```
models.Index(fields=['created_at']),
    ]
```

- **Database Sharding**: For extremely large datasets, consider database sharding, which splits the database into multiple parts, each storing a portion of the data. This can improve read and write performance by distributing the workload.

- **Query Optimization**: Use **select_related** and **prefetch_related** to avoid the N+1 query problem and optimize the retrieval of related data. Use `only()` and `defer()` to limit the fields loaded from the database.

4. Asynchronous Task Processing

Offload long-running or resource-intensive tasks to background workers. **Celery** is a popular choice for handling background tasks in Django. By using Celery, you can move tasks like sending emails, image processing, and other time-consuming processes out of the main request-response cycle.

```bash
pip install celery redis
```

Configure Celery to handle tasks asynchronously, allowing your web server to focus on handling requests while Celery takes care of the heavy lifting.

5. Optimizing Static and Media Files

- **Static File Serving**: Serve static files (CSS, JavaScript, images) through a web server like **Nginx** instead of Django. This reduces the load on your Django application and improves performance.
- **Use a CDN**: Serve static and media files via a Content Delivery Network (CDN) like **Cloudflare** or **AWS S3** for faster content delivery and to offload traffic from your server.

Maintaining and Updating Codebase

Maintaining a Django application involves fixing bugs, updating dependencies, and introducing new features while ensuring that the application remains secure and functional. Here are strategies for maintaining and updating your Django codebase:

1. Version Control with Git

Use **Git** for version control to manage changes to the codebase. Git helps track code changes, collaborate with teams, and roll back changes if needed.

- **Branching**: Use feature branches to isolate development work. Once the feature is complete, create a pull request (PR) for code review and merge it into the main branch (e.g., `master` or `main`).
- **Tagging Releases**: Tag important versions or releases in Git to keep track of stable versions of the application.

2. Regularly Update Dependencies

Keep your application's dependencies up to date to ensure you are using the latest features and security patches.

- Use **Dependabot** or **PyUp** to automate the process of keeping dependencies up to date and secure.
- Run `pip freeze` regularly to check for outdated packages.

3. Refactor Code for Maintainability

As your application grows, periodically refactor the code to improve its readability, performance, and maintainability. This includes:

- Splitting large views or functions into smaller, more manageable pieces.
- Moving reusable code into separate functions, classes, or modules.

- Ensuring that your models, views, and templates follow Django's best practices.

4. Write Tests and Run Them Regularly

Writing automated tests is essential for maintaining the reliability of the application. Django has a built-in testing framework that you can use to test models, views, forms, and more.

- **Test coverage**: Write unit tests, integration tests, and end-to-end tests to ensure your application behaves as expected.
- **Continuous Integration (CI)**: Use CI tools like **Travis CI**, **GitHub Actions**, or **CircleCI** to automatically run your tests whenever you push changes to your code repository.

5. Keep Documentation Up to Date

As you introduce new features or changes to the application, make sure to update the documentation accordingly. This includes both code documentation and user-facing documentation.

- **Docstrings**: Use Python docstrings to document functions, classes, and modules in your code.
- **README**: Keep the README.md file up to date with the latest setup instructions, environment variables, and features.

Handling Versioning, Databases, and Deployment

1. Handling Database Migrations

As your Django app evolves, the database schema will need to change. Django's migration system helps manage these changes.

- **Creating Migrations**: When you make changes to the models, run `python manage.py makemigrations` to generate the migration files.
- **Applying Migrations**: Use `python manage.py migrate` to apply migrations to the database.
- **Rollback Migrations**: Use `python manage.py migrate app_name <previous_migration>` to roll back migrations if needed.

2. Database Versioning

As the database schema changes over time, it's important to keep track of schema versions and avoid issues during deployment.

- **Use Data Migrations**: For changes that require altering or migrating data, you can create custom data migrations.

```python
python

from django.db import migrations
```

```
def populate_field(apps, schema_editor):
    MyModel = apps.get_model('myapp', 'MyModel')
    for obj in MyModel.objects.all():
        obj.new_field = 'default_value'
        obj.save()

class Migration(migrations.Migration):
    dependencies              =              [('myapp',
'previous_migration')]
    operations = [
        migrations.RunPython(populate_field),
    ]
```

3. Deployment Strategies

When deploying changes to a Django application, ensure that the deployment process is smooth, reliable, and consistent across environments.

- **Zero Downtime Deployments**: Use deployment strategies like **blue-green deployment** or **canary releases** to ensure that the app remains available during updates.
- **Rolling Deployments**: For large applications, use rolling deployments to gradually deploy changes across multiple servers, ensuring high availability.

- **Environment Variables**: Use environment variables for sensitive information (e.g., API keys, database credentials) instead of hardcoding them in the codebase.
- **Use Docker**: Containerize your application using Docker to ensure consistency between development, staging, and production environments.

4. Automate Deployment with CI/CD

Set up **Continuous Integration (CI)** and **Continuous Deployment (CD)** pipelines to automate the process of testing, building, and deploying your Django app.

- **CI Tools**: Use tools like **GitHub Actions, GitLab CI**, or **Jenkins** to automate testing and deployment.
- **Deployment Tools**: Use tools like **Docker**, **Ansible**, or **Terraform** to automate deployment processes.

Example: A typical deployment pipeline includes:

1. Pushing code to a Git repository.
2. Running tests automatically with CI tools.
3. Building and packaging the application (e.g., using Docker).
4. Deploying the application to a staging or production server.

Summary

In this chapter, we explored advanced topics for **scaling** and **maintaining** Django applications, which are critical as your app grows. We covered:

- **Scaling strategies**: Horizontal scaling with load balancing, database replication, caching, and background task handling with Celery.
- **Maintaining the codebase**: Using Git for version control, refactoring code, keeping dependencies up to date, writing automated tests, and maintaining documentation.
- **Handling versioning, databases, and deployment**: Managing database migrations, versioning, and implementing deployment strategies for zero downtime and automation with CI/CD tools.

By following these best practices and strategies, you can scale and maintain your Django application efficiently while ensuring its performance and stability as it grows.